essentials

Produced by **ACP**books

Printed by Bookbuilders, China.
Published by ACP Publishing Pty Limited, 54 Park Street, Sydney, NSW 2000 (GPO Box 4088, Sydney, NSW 2001),
phone (02) 9282 8618, fax (02) 9267 9438, acpbooks@acp.com.au www.acpbooks.com.au
AUSTRALIA: Distributed by Network Services, GPO Box 4088, Sydney, NSW 2001, phone (02) 9282 8777, fax (02) 9264 3278.
UNITED KINGDOM: Distributed by Australian Consolidated Press (UK), Moulton Park Business Centre, Red House Road,
Moulton Park, Northampton, NN3 6AQ, phone (01604) 497 531, fax (01604) 497 533, acpukltd@aol.com
CANADA: Distributed by Whitecap Books Ltd, 351 Lynn Avenue, North Vancouver, BC, V7J 2C4,
phone (604) 980 9852, fax (604) 980 8197, customerservice@whitecap.ca www.whitecap.ca
NEW ZEALAND: Distributed by Netlink Distribution Company, ACP Media Centre, Cnr Fanshawe and Beaumont Streets,
Westhaven, Auckland (PO Box 47906, Ponsonby, Auckland, NZ), phone (09) 366 9966, ask@ndcnz.co.nz

Gourmet essentials.
Includes index.
ISBN 1 86396 358 8.
1. Cookery. I. Australian Gourmet Traveller.
641.5
© ACP Publishing Pty Limited 2004
ABN 18 053 273 546

AUSTRALIAN GOURMET TRAVELLER
Group publisher Phil Scott
Editorial director Andy Harris
Editor Judy Sarris
Food editor Leanne Kitchen
Deputy food editor Sophia Young
Assistant food editors Christine Osmond, Kathleen Gandy

ACP BOOKS
Editorial director Susan Tomnay
Creative director Hieu Chi Nguyen
Senior editor Lynda Wilton
Publishing manager (sales) Brian Cearnes
Publishing manager (rights & new projects) Jane Hazell
Brand manager Donna Gianniotis
Production manager Carol Currie
Business manager Seymour Cohen
Assistant business analyst Martin Howes
Studio manager Caryl Wiggins
Pre-press Harry Palmer
Editorial & sales coordinator Caroline Lowry
Editorial assistant Karen Lai

Photographer Ben Dearnley
Stylist Kirsty Cassidy
Recipes by Vanessa Broadfoot, Ross Dobson,
Rodney Dunn, Kathleen Gandy, Leanne Kitchen,
Lynne Mullins, Christine Osmond, Sophia Young
Food preparation by Christine Sheppard

Chief executive officer John Alexander
Group publisher Pat Ingram
Publisher Sue Wannan

THANKS TO THESE STOCKISTS AND SUPPLIERS
Accoutrement, phone (02) 9969 1031 or (02) 9418 2992
The Art of Wine & Food, phone (02) 9363 2817
The Bay Tree, phone (02) 9328 1101
Bayswiss, phone (02) 9326 0111
Beclau Design Furniture, phone (02) 9698 6422
Bed, Bath & Table, phone (02) 9960 3366
Bisanna Tiles, phone (02) 9310 2500
Bison Homewares, phone (02) 6284 2334
Boxx, phone (02) 9280 1878
Camargue, phone (02) 9960 6234
Cloth new Australian fabric, phone (02) 9664 5570
Country Road Homewear, phone 1800 801 911
David Edmonds, phone 0419 611 026
Design Mode International, phone (02) 9998 8200
Demcos Seafoods, phone (02) 9700 9000
The Essential Ingredient, phone (02) 9550 5477
Les Olivades, phone (02) 9327 8073
Lucienne Linens, phone (02) 9969 4946
Milner's (Le Creuset), phone 1800 099 266
Mrs Red & Sons, phone (02) 9310 4860
Mud Australia, phone (02) 9518 0220
Murdoch Produce, phone (02) 9517 9499
NSW Leather Co, phone (02) 9319 2900
Orrefors Kosta Boda (head office), phone (02) 9913 4200
Orson & Blake, phone (02) 9326 1155
Papaya, phone (02) 9362 1620
Peter's of Kensington, phone (02) 9662 1099
Poliform Australia, phone (02) 9690 0777
Porter's Original Paints, phone (02) 9698 5322
Robert Burton, phone (02) 9332 2944
Simon Johnson Purveyor of Quality Foods, phone 1800 655 522
Spence & Lyda, phone (02) 9212 6747
Vic's Premium Quality Meat, phone (02) 9667 3922
Wheel & Barrow, phone (02) 9938 4555

AUSTRALIAN GOURMET TRAVELLER

essentials

ACPbooks

contents

introduction

Cooking is a derivative craft. By mastering some basic techniques and refining a repertoire of useful dishes, the cook can equip himself or herself with all the building blocks needed for further possibilities. Once one basic recipe has been conquered, it can often be subtly adjusted, or used as a base for myriad other dishes. This is the rationale behind *Australian Gourmet Traveller ESSENTIALS*: to present practical and adaptable recipes that are not only fabulous as they are, but provide the starting point for added inspiration. When you understand, for example, how to make an egg-based, baked savoury custard, you can go on to modify ingredients and cooking procedures to give a host of different results. Vary flavour profiles (with sun-dried tomato and basil, saffron and prawns, or spinach and lemon, for example) to give a simple, elegant dinner party entrée or a light lunch with salad. With the addition of cheese and perhaps some asparagus, that same custard mixture can be used as a filling for quiche or, when flavoured with mushrooms and asiago and baked over bread, will become a satisfying savoury bread pudding – perfect casual fare. Similarly, oven-poached quinces, while delicious on their own with some whipped cream to the side, can easily be incorporated into a lush upside-down cake or a warming clafoutis. Thus, with this book, the *Australian Gourmet Traveller* team gives you not only a definitive collection of essential recipes, but also inventive ways to extend or to vary each of them.

BRAISED ARTICHOKES

THIS VEGETABLE FAVOURITE IS MADE TENDER BY OLIVE OIL AND PERFUMED WITH LEMON AND THYME

BASE RECIPE

10 globe artichokes
Juice and finely grated rind of 1 lemon
½ cup olive oil
6 cloves of garlic, thinly sliced
10 sprigs of thyme, plus extra sprigs, to serve
Olives, prosciutto, grissini and bread, optional, to serve

Trim artichoke stalks to 2cm, snap off tough outer leaves until you reach tender pale leaves, then, using a small sharp knife, carefully trim bases, cutting down the length of the stem to remove the outside of the stalk. Trim 2cm from top of each artichoke and cut into quarters lengthways. Using a teaspoon, scoop out hairy choke and discard, placing trimmed artichokes in a large bowl of water combined with lemon juice, as you go.

Heat olive oil in a large saucepan, add garlic and thyme and cook over medium heat for 1 minute, then add drained artichokes and stir for 5 minutes or until artichokes start to soften. Add lemon rind and ⅓ cup water, season to taste, then reduce heat to low and cook, covered, for 40 minutes or until artichokes are tender. Serve drained artichokes, scattered with extra thyme sprigs, as part of an antipasti selection with olives, prosciutto, grissini and bread, or use in one of the following recipes.
Serves 4-6

Artichoke, thyme and pearl barley risotto

200g (1 cup) pearl barley
1.75 litres chicken stock
2 tablespoons olive oil
1 onion, finely chopped
200g (1 cup) vialone nano or other risotto rice
250ml dry white wine
40g (½ cup) finely grated parmesan
1 quantity braised artichokes, drained
Small sprigs of thyme and shaved parmesan, to serve

Place pearl barley in a bowl, cover with water and stand for 3 hours, then drain. Bring stock to the boil in a saucepan over low heat and keep at a gentle simmer. Heat olive oil in a large saucepan over medium-high heat, add onion and stir over medium heat for 5 minutes or until soft. Add rice and stir for 2 minutes or until rice is well coated in oil, then add drained barley and stir to combine. Add wine and stir until nearly evaporated, then add hot stock, a cupful at a time, stirring frequently, allowing each addition to be absorbed before adding the next. When rice is al dente and barley is cooked, add parmesan and artichokes and season to taste, then divide among bowls and serve immediately, scattered with sprigs of thyme and shaved parmesan.
Serves 4

Artichoke and feta pastries

1 small spanish onion, finely chopped
½ quantity braised artichokes, drained and
    coarsely chopped
170g goat's feta, crumbled
9 sheets of filo pastry
60g butter, melted
Lemon wedges, to serve

Combine onion, artichokes and feta in a bowl and
season to taste. Place filo pastry on a dry surface and
cover with a clean tea towel. Layer 3 sheets of filo pastry,
brushing each layer except top with melted butter.
Using a sharp knife, cut pastry widthways into
4, then cut in half lengthways to make eight 11x14cm
rectangles. Spread 1 tablespoon of mixture lengthways
along centre of each rectangle, leaving a 1cm border.
Starting at a long side, roll each piece of pastry into
a cigar shape, folding in ends to enclose filling, then
place on baking paper-lined oven trays. Do not roll
pastries too tightly or they may burst. Repeat with
remaining pastry, butter and filling. Brush pastries
all over with melted butter, then bake at 180C for
12 minutes or until golden. Serve warm or at room
temperature with lemon wedges.
Makes 24

MAYONNAISE

TRUE MAYONNAISE TRANSFORMS OTHER DISHES WITH ITS SUPERIOR TEXTURE AND LUXURIOUS TASTE

BASE RECIPE

3 egg yolks
2 teaspoons Dijon mustard
1 tablespoon lemon juice
300ml olive oil

Process egg yolks, mustard and lemon juice in a food processor until combined, then, with motor running, add olive oil in a thin stream until emulsified and thick. Season to taste, then add 1-2 teaspoons of boiling water to thin mayonnaise, if necessary, stirring to combine well. Cover closely with plastic wrap and refrigerate until needed. Mayonnaise will keep refrigerated for up to 1 week.
Makes about 1½ cups

Add one of the following combinations of ingredients to 1 quantity mayonnaise.

Fresh tomato-chilli mayonnaise: Process mayonnaise with 1 peeled, seeded and finely chopped egg tomato and 1 finely chopped fresh small red chilli until well combined and smooth.

Olive mayonnaise: 2½ tablespoons finely chopped pitted kalamata olives.

Rocket mayonnaise: Process 1 bunch blanched and drained rocket leaves and ¼ cup blanched and drained basil leaves with 1 quantity mayonnaise until well combined and smooth.

Lime mayonnaise: Substitute lemon juice with 2 tablespoons lime juice and add finely grated rind of 1 lime.

Sauce gribiche: 2 tablespoons chopped capers, 6 coarsely chopped cornichons, 2 teaspoons Dijon mustard and 1 tablespoon each chopped chervil, finely chopped chives and tarragon.

Facing page, mayonnaise varieties clockwise from left: fresh tomato-chilli, olive, rocket, lime, sauce gribiche

Fish tacos with lime and coriander coleslaw

450g savoy cabbage (about ¼ head), shredded
450g red cabbage (about ¼ head), shredded
6 pieces of blue-eye (about 180g each), or other firm,
   white-fleshed fish fillets
Olive oil
1 teaspoon cayenne
1½ cups (firmly packed) coriander leaves (about 1 bunch)
4 green onions, thinly sliced
½ cup lime mayonnaise
12 flour tortillas
Lime wedges and sour cream, to serve

Combine cabbage with 1 teaspoon sea salt in a bowl
and set aside for 20 minutes.

Meanwhile, brush fish with olive oil, season to taste
and sprinkle on both sides with a little cayenne.
Barbecue or char-grill fish for 3-4 minutes on each side
or until just cooked through. Stand fish for 5 minutes,
then break into large flakes.

Combine cabbage, coriander, green onions and lime
mayonnaise in a bowl and season to taste. Barbecue or
char-grill tortillas, in batches, for 30 seconds on each
side or until just warm and lightly golden, then transfer
to a plate, cover with a tea towel and keep warm. Serve
warm tortillas, lime and coriander coleslaw, flaked fish,
lime wedges and sour cream separately for guests to
assemble their own tacos.

Serves 4-6

Gratinéed mussels

800g small black mussels, scrubbed and bearded
2 tablespoons chopped dill
1 egg yolk
1½ tablespoons Pernod or pastis (such as Ricard)
¾ cup mayonnaise
Crusty bread, optional, to serve

Bring ½ cup water to the boil in a large frying pan,
add half the mussels and cook, covered, for 3-4 minutes
or just until shells open. Remove and repeat with
remaining mussels. Discard any unopened mussels,
then remove top shell and place mussels in the half
shell on an oven tray. Combine dill, egg yolk, Pernod
and mayonnaise in a bowl, then spread 2-3 teaspoons
of mayonnaise mixture over each mussel. Place under
a medium-hot grill for 2-3 minutes or just until
mussels are warmed and lightly browned,
then serve immediately with crusty bread, if using.
Serves 4-6

ONION CONFIT

PATIENT COOKING RENDERS ONIONS SWEET AND STICKY – GREAT IN SOUP, A TART OR OVER LAMB

BASE RECIPE

¼ cup olive oil

1kg onions, halved and thinly sliced

2 cloves of garlic, finely chopped

1 fresh bay leaf

1 teaspoon finely chopped rosemary

1 teaspoon finely chopped thyme

1 anchovy fillet, finely chopped, optional

60ml red wine

1 teaspoon red wine vinegar

½ teaspoon brown sugar

Heat olive oil in a large heavy-based frying pan, add onions, garlic, herbs and anchovy, if using, and mix well. Cook, covered, over low heat for 1 hour or until onions are golden, stirring frequently to prevent burning.

Stir in remaining ingredients, then cook over low heat for another 20 minutes or until liquid has reduced and onions are glossy. Season to taste. Cool. Onion confit will keep, refrigerated, in an airtight container for up to 2 weeks.

Makes about 2 cups

Lamb, onion confit and watercress rolls

4 sourdough rolls

10g soft butter

2 lamb backstraps
   (about 200g each), trimmed

1 tablespoon olive oil

½ cup picked watercress sprigs

½ cup baby endive leaves

⅓ cup onion confit

Cut rolls almost in half widthways, leaving one side intact, then spread lightly with butter.

Brush lamb backstraps with olive oil and season to taste, then char-grill for 3-4 minutes on each side for medium or until cooked to your liking. Rest lamb for 2-3 minutes, then cut on the diagonal into 1cm-thick slices.

Divide watercress, baby endive and lamb among rolls, then top with a spoonful of onion confit.

Serves 4

French onion soup

1 quantity onion confit
1 tablespoon plain flour
125ml red wine
1 litre beef stock
8 thin slices of baguette
1 clove of garlic, halved
60g gruyère, grated

Place onion confit in a heavy-based saucepan and stir over medium heat until heated through, then add flour and stir for 3 minutes. Add wine and simmer for 5 minutes or until reduced by half. Add stock and simmer over low heat for 10 minutes, then season to taste.

Place baguette slices on an oven tray and toast under a hot grill, then, while hot, rub both sides with a cut side of garlic clove. Sprinkle with gruyère, then cook under a hot grill until cheese melts and bubbles. Divide soup among warmed bowls and top with gruyère croûtons.

Serves 4

Onion confit tart

1 sheet of frozen butter puff pastry, thawed
1 egg yolk, combined with 1 tablespoon milk
1 cup onion confit
100g soft goat's cheese, crumbled
90g (½ cup) Ligurian olives or other
    small black olives, pitted
¼ cup basil leaves, torn
1 tablespoon extra virgin olive oil
Radicchio and baby endive leaves
    dressed with lemon and olive oil, optional, to serve

Place pastry sheet on a baking paper-lined oven tray, then turn each edge over by 1cm and press down lightly to form a raised border. Prick centre of pastry all over with a fork, then brush border with a little egg mixture.

Spread onion confit evenly over pastry, then scatter with goat's cheese and olives. Scatter basil leaves over tart and drizzle with olive oil. Season to taste and bake at 200C for 20 minutes or until pastry is golden and crisp. Serve tart warm or at room temperature with radicchio and baby endive salad, if using.
Serves 4

SOFT POLENTA

POLENTA BEGS FOR ASSERTIVE PARTNERS, FROM HEADY BEETROOT RELISH TO SWEETLY SPICED PEAR

BASE RECIPE

2 cups water, chicken or vegetable stock
2 cups milk
1 onion, peeled and halved
2 cloves of garlic, bruised
2 fresh bay leaves
180g (1 cup) polenta
20g butter
2 tablespoons grated parmesan
Sautéed field mushrooms and wilted spinach, optional, to serve

Place water or stock, milk, onion, garlic and bay leaves in a heavy-based saucepan and bring almost to the boil. Remove from heat, cover and stand for 30 minutes for flavours to infuse. Strain, return milk mixture to a clean saucepan and bring almost to the boil, then slowly pour in polenta, whisking continuously until well combined. Reduce heat to very low, then cook for 30 minutes or until the consistency of soft porridge, stirring with a wooden spoon every few minutes to prevent burning. Remove from heat, stir in butter and parmesan, then season to taste and serve immediately, spooned into bowls, with sautéed mushrooms and wilted spinach to the side, if using.
Serves 4

Fontina polenta: Stir 150g grated fontina into hot polenta until melted.

Sweet polenta: Follow the base recipe for soft polenta using water and milk, omitting onion, garlic, bay leaves and parmesan. Add 1 cinnamon stick and ½ vanilla bean, split lengthways, to liquid. When polenta is thick, remove from heat and stir in ⅓ cup honey, ¼ cup crème fraîche and a pinch of freshly grated nutmeg.

Polenta canapés with duck breast and beetroot relish

1 quantity hot soft polenta
2 tablespoons olive oil
1 cooked duck breast fillet, or 1 smoked
    chicken breast fillet, thinly sliced widthways
⅓ cup picked watercress sprigs
Beetroot relish
250g beetroot, peeled and grated
1 tablespoon red wine vinegar
1 tablespoon brown sugar
¼ teaspoon mustard powder
2 tablespoons raisins

Pour soft polenta into a greased 17x30cm shallow tray, cover and refrigerate for 2 hours or until firm. Turn out onto a board and, using a 4cm pastry cutter, cut out 30 rounds. Heat olive oil in a non-stick frying pan and cook polenta, in batches, over medium heat for 3 minutes on each side or until golden and crisp, then drain on absorbent paper.

For beetroot relish, place all ingredients and ¼ cup water in a small heavy-based saucepan and bring to the boil. Reduce heat to low and simmer, covered, for 30 minutes, then uncover and simmer for another 20 minutes or until thick. Remove from heat and season to taste. Cool.

Meanwhile, top each polenta round with a slice of duck breast, teaspoonfuls of beetroot relish and a sprig of watercress.

Makes 30

Sweet soft polenta with dried pear compote

1 quantity hot sweet polenta
Dried pear compote
200g dried pears
75g (⅓ cup) caster sugar
1 star anise, plus extra, to serve
5cm strip of orange rind, cut into julienne
½ vanilla bean, split lengthways

For dried pear compote, place pears in a heatproof bowl, cover with 3 cups of boiling water and stand for 1 hour, then strain liquid into a heavy-based saucepan and reserve pears. Add sugar, star anise, orange rind, scraped seeds from vanilla bean and bean to pan, bring to a simmer, stirring to dissolve sugar, then cook, covered, over low heat for 10 minutes. Add soaked pears and simmer, covered, over low heat for 20 minutes or until pears are very soft.

Divide sweet polenta between 4 plates, spoon over warm or room-temperature dried pear compote, and top with an extra star anise.

Serves 4

GRAVLAX

CURING IN SUGAR, SALT AND AROMATICS LENDS A WORLD OF POSSIBILITIES TO SEA-FRESH SALMON

BASE RECIPE

Recipe can be halved.

1 teaspoon black peppercorns
10 juniper berries
120g caster sugar
90g flaked sea salt
3kg ocean trout or salmon, cleaned, filleted and pin-boned
2 bunches of dill, sprigs removed
2 tablespoons Pernod or pastis (such as Ricard)

Combine spices and sugar in a mortar and crush with
a pestle until coarsely ground, then stir in salt. Place
1 fish fillet, skin-side down, on a stainless steel or plastic
tray and sprinkle with half the spice mixture, top with dill
and remaining spice mixture, then drizzle with Pernod.
Place the second fillet on top, flesh-side down, and
cover with plastic wrap, then place a small chopping
board over fish, place weights or food cans evenly on
chopping board and refrigerate.

Every 12 hours for 2-3 days, unwrap fish, separate fillets
and spoon liquid over, then replace fillets, re-cover and
weight again.

Scrape away most of the curing mixture and pat gravlax
dry with absorbent paper. Using a very sharp knife, cut
gravlax at a 45-degree angle into thin slices and use in one
of the following recipes. Gravlax will keep, refrigerated,
in plastic wrap for up to 2 weeks.
Serves 20

Gravlax with mustard honey sauce, rye bread and rocket

12 slices of gravlax
8 slices of rye bread
2 cups rocket leaves
Lemon wedges, to serve
Mustard honey sauce
⅓ cup Dijon mustard
2 tablespoons honey
2 tablespoons finely chopped dill
2 tablespoons olive oil

For mustard honey sauce, combine all ingredients
and 2 tablespoons water and season to taste.
Makes 150ml mustard honey sauce.

Serve slices of gravlax with mustard honey
sauce, slices of rye bread, rocket and lemon wedges
passed separately.
Serves 4 as an entrée or a snack

Witlof, avocado and fennel salad with seared gravlax

1 avocado, sliced
1 small bulb of fennel, trimmed and very thinly sliced
2 lebanese cucumbers, peeled, seeded and
    thinly sliced on the diagonal
2 witlof, bases trimmed and leaves separated
Olive oil
8 slices (5mm thick) of gravlax
Lime dressing
Finely grated rind and juice of 1 lime
¼ cup olive oil
2 teaspoons rice vinegar

For lime dressing, place all ingredients and a pinch of sugar in a bowl, then season to taste and whisk to combine.

Combine avocado, fennel, cucumbers and witlof in a bowl, add dressing and toss gently to combine, then divide salad among 4 plates. Heat a little oil in a heavy-based frying pan and cook gravlax slices, in batches, for 30 seconds on each side or until just changed in colour, then place on top of salads. Serve immediately.
Serves 4

Gravlax tarts with cucumber and horseradish

2 lebanese cucumbers, peeled, seeded and thinly sliced
1 sheet of frozen puff pastry, thawed
½ small spanish onion, thinly sliced
Olive oil
½ cup sour cream
1 tablespoon horseradish cream
12 thin slices of gravlax (about 125g)
¼ cup (loosely packed) chervil sprigs

Toss cucumbers with 1 teaspoon sea salt in a colander over a bowl, stand for 30 minutes, then rinse under water and pat dry with absorbent paper.

Using an 11cm pastry cutter, cut 4 rounds from pastry sheet and place on a greased oven tray, then prick pastry all over with a fork. Scatter with onion, leaving a 5mm border, then season to taste and drizzle with a little olive oil. Bake at 220C for 12-15 minutes or until pastry is golden and crisp, then cool for 10 minutes.

Meanwhile, combine sour cream and horseradish cream in a bowl and season to taste, then divide mixture between tarts. Top with cucumber, then slices of gravlax and chervil sprigs. Sprinkle with freshly ground black pepper and serve immediately.

Makes 4 tarts

PEPERONATA

CAPSICUM AND TOMATO MELT INTO A LUSH MIXTURE IDEAL IN SALADS, ON CROSTINI OR WITH FISH

BASE RECIPE

2 red capsicum

2 yellow capsicum

⅓ cup olive oil

2 onions, halved and thinly sliced

2 cloves of garlic, finely chopped

4 egg tomatoes, peeled and coarsely chopped

2 tablespoons finely chopped sultanas

1 teaspoon red wine vinegar

Halve capsicum, remove seeds and cut into 1cm strips. Heat olive oil in a large heavy-based saucepan, add onions and 1½ teaspoons sea salt and cook, stirring occasionally, over medium heat for 10 minutes or until soft. Add capsicum and garlic and cook for 10 minutes. Add tomatoes and sultanas, bring to a simmer and cook over low-medium heat for 25 minutes or until capsicum is very soft and tomatoes are pulpy. Stir in red wine vinegar and season to taste.

Peperonata will keep refrigerated for up to 1 week.

Makes about 1 litre

Peperonata on bruschetta with anchovies

8 slices of Italian-style bread

1 clove of garlic, bruised

2 tablespoons olive oil

1 cup peperonata

8 anchovy fillets

Rub bread all over with garlic and brush both sides with olive oil, then cook under a hot grill until golden on both sides. Spoon a little peperonata over each warm bruschetta and top with an anchovy fillet.

Serves 4

Lemon and thyme grilled barramundi with peperonata and grilled potatoes

600g desiree potatoes
4 cleaned barramundi (about 400g each)
Olive oil
2 lemons, each cut into 6
8 sprigs of thyme
3 green onions, finely chopped
Grated rind of 1 lemon
1 quantity peperonata

Place potatoes in a saucepan, cover with water and bring to the boil, simmer for 10 minutes and drain (potatoes will still be firm). Cool, then cut potatoes into 3mm-thick slices.

Brush fish well with olive oil, stuff cavities with lemon and thyme and season to taste. Wrap tails in oiled foil, then barbecue fish, on the hottest part of the grill to prevent skin from sticking, for 5 minutes on each side or until cooked, then rest in a warm place for 5 minutes.

Meanwhile, brush potatoes with olive oil, season to taste and barbecue on each side for 1-2 minutes or until tender. Combine potatoes with green onions, lemon rind and 2 tablespoons olive oil and season to taste.

Serve barramundi on potatoes with room-temperature peperonata to the side.
Serves 4

Panzanella

This Tuscan salad makes a wonderful entrée or accompaniment to roast and grilled chicken, lamb or beef.

3 vine-ripened tomatoes,
    peeled, seeded and cut into wedges
80g small black olives
2 tablespoons drained capers
½ Italian-style day-old loaf of bread,
    crusts removed, torn into 3cm pieces
¼ cup torn basil leaves
1 tablespoon red wine vinegar
2 tablespoons extra virgin olive oil
1 quantity peperonata

Combine all ingredients in a large bowl, season to taste and toss gently to combine. Divide salad among bowls and serve.
Serves 4

RISOTTO

BASE RECIPE

1 litre chicken stock
125ml dry white or dry red wine
100g butter, chopped
¼ cup olive oil
1 small onion, finely chopped
2 cloves of garlic, coarsely chopped
300g (1½ cups) arborio rice
20g (¼ cup) finely grated parmesan, optional

Place stock and white wine (or red wine if making red wine, pumpkin and rosemary risotto) in a saucepan, bring to a simmer over medium heat and keep at a gentle simmer.

Heat half the butter and oil in a heavy-based saucepan, add onion and garlic and cook for 5 minutes or until onion is soft. Add rice and stir for 2 minutes or until well coated in oil. Add 1 cup hot stock and stir over medium heat until stock is absorbed. Add remaining stock, a cupful at a time, stirring frequently, allowing each addition to be absorbed before adding the next. Add remaining butter and parmesan, if using, then season to taste and stir until butter is melted. Serve immediately.

Makes about 1 litre. Serves 4

Cabbage, pancetta and gorgonzola risotto: Heat 1 tablespoon olive oil in a frying pan, add 150g pancetta cut into 6mm pieces and stir over medium heat for 5 minutes. Add 400g finely shredded white cabbage (about ¼ cabbage) and mix well, then cook, covered, for 10 minutes. Season to taste, then stir into risotto with 40g crumbled gorgonzola picante and serve immediately, scattered with 2 tablespoons finely chopped flat-leaf parsley.

Red wine, pumpkin and rosemary risotto: Cut 450g peeled and seeded Queensland blue pumpkin into 1cm pieces and toss with 1½ teaspoons rosemary leaves and 1 tablespoon olive oil in a roasting pan. Season to taste, then roast at 190C for 35 minutes or until tender. Stir mixture into risotto made with red wine and serve immediately.

Lemon, fennel, chive and scallop risotto: Heat 30g butter in a frying pan and cook 1 finely chopped bulb of baby fennel over medium heat for 5 minutes or until tender, then season to taste. Stir into risotto, omitting parmesan, with finely grated rind of 1 lemon and 2 tablespoons finely chopped chives. Heat 30g butter in a frying pan and cook 400g scallops, in batches, for 1 minute on each side or until just tender. Serve risotto immediately, topped with scallops.

Facing page, cabbage, pancetta and gorgonzola risotto

Stuffed squid

1⅓ cups cooled risotto
80g (½ cup) pinenuts, lightly roasted
2 tablespoons chopped dill
⅓ cup chopped flat-leaf parsley
16 small squid (8-10cm long), cleaned
Olive oil
4 vine-ripened tomatoes, cut into 6mm-thick slices
½ spanish onion, thinly sliced
¼ cup oregano leaves
2 tablespoons dry white wine

Combine risotto with pinenuts, dill and half the parsley in a small bowl, fill each squid tube three-quarters full (approximately 1 tablespoon mixture), then secure top with a toothpick.

Drizzle 22x28cm ceramic baking dish with olive oil, then place tomatoes in a single layer over base, scatter with onion and oregano leaves, and season to taste. Place stuffed squid tubes in a single layer on top, drizzle with wine and 2 tablespoons olive oil, then bake at 180C for 40 minutes or until tender. Serve immediately, sprinkled with remaining parsley.
Serves 4

Rice and seafood soup

2 tablespoons olive oil
1 onion, finely chopped
Pinch of saffron threads
2 cloves of garlic, coarsely chopped
½ teaspoon cumin seeds
½ teaspoon smoked hot Spanish paprika
1 litre fish stock
1 tablespoon tomato paste
1 cup cooled risotto, omitting parmesan
200g skinless ocean trout fillet,
    pin-boned and cut into 2-3cm pieces
8 medium green prawns, peeled and
    cleaned with tails intact
2 red capsicum, quartered, seeded, grilled
    until blackened, peeled and thinly sliced
4 egg tomatoes, peeled, seeded and chopped
8 scallops
¼ cup coarsely chopped coriander leaves

Heat olive oil in a large saucepan, add onion and saffron
and cook, stirring occasionally, over medium heat for
5 minutes. Add garlic, cumin seeds and paprika and
cook for 1-2 minutes or until fragrant. Add stock, tomato
paste, risotto and 1 cup water, combine well and bring
to the boil. Add fish, prawns, capsicum and tomatoes
and cook over medium heat for 5 minutes. Add scallops
and coriander and stir to combine, then cook for
2 minutes or until scallops are just tender. Season
to taste, then serve in warm bowls.
Serves 4

SAVOURY CUSTARD

SILKY CUSTARD IS EQUALLY AT HOME IN A QUICHE, A SAVOURY PUDDING OR BAKED IN A RAMEKIN

BASE RECIPE

1½ cups pouring cream
½ cup milk
½ onion
1 clove of garlic
1 dried bay leaf
6 egg yolks
2 eggs
Mâche (lamb's lettuce) salad, optional, to serve

Combine cream, milk, onion, garlic and bay leaf in a small heavy-based saucepan and bring almost to the boil, then remove from heat, cover and stand for 30 minutes for flavours to develop. Strain mixture into a bowl, discarding solids. Whisk yolks and eggs together in a bowl until combined, then stir into milk mixture until well combined. Add ingredients for one of the variations listed, season to taste and mix well. Divide mixture among 6 lightly greased ½-cup-capacity timbale moulds or heatproof cups, making sure chopped ingredients are evenly distributed, then place moulds in a roasting pan and pour in enough boiling water to come halfway up sides of moulds. Bake at 140C for 30-35 minutes or until custard is just set. Stand custards in water bath until cooled, then refrigerate for at least 2 hours. Run a small knife around edge of custards and gently turn out onto plates or serve straight from cups with a mâche salad, if using.

Makes 6

Add one of the following combinations of ingredients to the base recipe, combine well and cook as before.

Sun-dried tomato and basil custards: Add 1 tablespoon finely chopped basil and 50g finely chopped sun-dried tomatoes to base recipe.

Saffron custards with prawns and salmon roe: Combine a pinch of saffron threads with 1 tablespoon dry white wine and stand for 10 minutes, then stir into base recipe. Finely chop 200g cooked and cleaned prawns and top each cooked custard with a small spoonful, then divide 30g salmon roe between tops.

Spinach and lemon custards: Blanch 120g baby spinach leaves in boiling salted water, then drain immediately and refresh in iced water, then drain again. Squeeze excess water from spinach, then chop very finely. Add chopped blanched spinach with finely grated rind of 1 lemon to base recipe.

Facing page, sun-dried tomato and basil custards

Asparagus and fontina quiche

250g asparagus, trimmed
2 tablespoons olive oil
1 quantity savoury custard mixture
150g fontina or gruyère, grated
2 tablespoons chopped flat-leaf parsley
Green salad, to serve
Pastry
200g (1⅓ cups) plain flour
120g cold unsalted butter, chopped

For pastry, process flour, butter and a pinch of salt in a food processor until mixture resembles coarse breadcrumbs. Add ¼ cup iced water and process until pastry just comes together. Form pastry into a disc, then wrap in plastic wrap and refrigerate for at least 2 hours.

Roll out pastry on a lightly floured surface and line a 24cm tart tin with removable base, prick base all over with a fork, then cover and refrigerate for 1 hour. Line pastry with baking paper, fill with dried beans or rice and bake at 200C for 20 minutes, then remove paper and beans, reduce oven temperature to 180C and bake for another 5 minutes or until pastry is crisp and golden. Cool.

Meanwhile, place asparagus on an oven tray, toss with olive oil and season to taste, then roast at 200C for 10-15 minutes or until tender. Cool.

Place asparagus in cooked tart shell, then combine savoury custard mixture with fontina and parsley and pour over asparagus. Bake at 160C for 25-30 minutes or until custard is just set. Stand quiche for 20 minutes before cutting. Serve slices with a green salad.
Serves 6

Swiss brown and porcini mushroom bread pudding

1 quantity savoury custard mixture
200g asiago or parmesan, grated
25g dried porcini mushrooms,
    soaked in boiling water for 30 minutes
80g butter, chopped
1 tablespoon olive oil
400g swiss brown mushrooms, sliced
2 tablespoons chopped marjoram
300g day-old sourdough bread, cut into 1cm slices

Combine savoury custard mixture and half the asiago
and season to taste. Drain porcini and squeeze out
excess water, then thinly slice. Heat 20g butter and olive
oil in a large heavy-based frying pan until foaming, then
add swiss brown and porcini mushrooms and cook over
medium heat for 8 minutes or until golden. Remove
from heat and stir in half the marjoram.

Lightly butter bread slices on both sides and layer
with mushroom mixture in a greased 1.5-litre baking
dish, then pour custard over. Sprinkle with remaining
asiago and marjoram, then dot with remaining butter.
Stand mixture for 20 minutes to allow custard to soak
into bread, then bake at 180C for 30-35 minutes or until
golden and set. Stand bread pudding for 10 minutes
before serving.
Serves 4-6

BREAD DOUGH

IMPRESS GUESTS WITH HOMEMADE BREAD ROLLS, A SWEET YEASTED CAKE OR AN EARTHY PIZZA

BASE RECIPE

7g dried yeast
2 tablespoons extra virgin olive oil, plus extra, for greasing
600g (4 cups) plain flour

Combine a pinch of sugar and ¼ cup warm water in a small bowl, sprinkle over yeast and stand for 7 minutes or until mixture is foamy. Combine yeast mixture, oil and another 1¼ cups warm water in a large bowl, add flour, then stir to form a dough. Turn out onto a lightly floured surface and knead for 10 minutes or until smooth and elastic. Place in a large, oiled bowl and turn to coat, then cover with plastic wrap and leave in a draught-free place for 1 hour or until doubled in size. Knock down dough, then divide into 20 even-sized pieces. Roll each piece into a ball, then place on oiled oven trays and leave, covered with tea towels, in a draught-free place for 40 minutes or until well risen. Bake rolls at 200C for 20 minutes or until golden and hollow-sounding when tapped on the base. Transfer to a wire rack to cool.

Makes 20 rolls

Sweet bread dough: Substitute milk for water and 75g melted unsalted butter for olive oil. Add 75g (⅓ cup) caster sugar and 2 beaten egg yolks with flour.

Sage and pancetta rolls: Follow the base recipe for bread dough, then, after first rising, divide it in half and roll out one half on a floured surface to a 20x45cm rectangle. With a long side facing you, place 80g thinly sliced pancetta over dough, then scatter over 8 torn sage leaves. Roll dough up tightly from long side to form a log, then roll log gently to lengthen slightly. Cut log into 10 even-sized rounds, then place rounds 2cm apart on an oven tray, flattening slightly with your hand. Repeat with remaining half of dough, another 80g pancetta and 8 sage leaves, then cover rolls loosely and leave in a draught-free place for 1 hour or until risen. Bake rolls at 200C for 20 minutes or until golden and hollow-sounding when tapped on the base. Transfer to a wire rack to cool.

Makes 20 rolls

Facing page, sage and pancetta rolls

Walnut-cinnamon babka

1 quantity sweet bread dough
Icing sugar, for dusting
Walnut-cinnamon filling
300g walnut pieces, chopped
110g (½ cup) caster sugar
1 teaspoon ground cinnamon
1 egg white, lightly beaten

For walnut-cinnamon filling, process walnuts, sugar and cinnamon in a food processor until finely ground, then add egg white and process until mixture forms a paste.

Follow the base recipe for sweet bread dough, then, after first rising, roll out on a lightly floured surface until 23x48cm. Sprinkle filling over, leaving a 1.5cm border, roll dough up lengthways, then ease into a buttered 10-cup-capacity kugelhopf tin, pressing ends together to seal. Cover with a tea towel and leave in a draught-free place for 40 minutes or until doubled in size. Bake babka at 180C for 50 minutes or until golden and hollow-sounding when tapped. Cool babka in tin, then turn out, dust with icing sugar and serve slices with coffee. Babka is best served on day of making.
Serves 8-10

Sardine, silverbeet and artichoke pizza

1 quantity bread dough
Olive oil
1 clove of garlic, thinly sliced
2 onions, finely chopped
1kg silverbeet (1 bunch), washed, trimmed and sliced
80g (1 cup) grated parmesan
120g (¾ cup) kalamata olives, pitted
6 marinated artichoke halves, halved lengthways
12 butterflied sardines (about 480g)

Follow the base recipe for bread dough, then, after first rising, divide in half. On a floured surface, roll each half out to a 32cm round and place on lightly oiled 33cm pizza trays. Cover pizza bases loosely with a damp tea towel and set aside.

Heat ¼ cup olive oil in a large saucepan, add garlic and onions and stir for 5 minutes until onions are soft. Using a slotted spoon, transfer mixture to a small bowl. Add silverbeet to same pan and cook, covered, for 5 minutes or until leaves are wilted and stems begin to soften, then drain well, squeezing to remove excess liquid.

Sprinkle half the parmesan over pizza bases, scatter with onion mixture, then spread silverbeet over. Place olives, artichoke halves and sardines over silverbeet, sprinkle with remaining parmesan and season to taste. Bake pizzas at 240C for 15 minutes or until bases are golden and crisp.

Serves 6

BRANDADE

COMPLEX, SATISFYING BRANDADE NEEDS FEW EMBELLISHMENTS TO ALLOW ITS QUALITIES TO SHINE

BASE RECIPE

400g piece of salt cod, soaked in cold water in the
   refrigerator for 24-36 hours, changing the water 3-4 times
1 tablespoon lemon juice
2 sprigs of flat-leaf parsley
1 dried bay leaf
8 black peppercorns
2 cloves of garlic, chopped
2 slices of white bread, crusts removed,
   soaked in water for 1 minute, then squeezed dry
¼ cup milk
¼ cup olive oil
Sliced rustic-style bread, to serve

Drain salt cod and place in a wide saucepan with lemon juice, parsley, bay
leaf, peppercorns and enough water to cover. Bring to the boil over high heat,
then reduce heat to low and simmer, covered, for 15 minutes. Drain cod, cool
slightly, remove and discard skin and bones, then break flesh into coarse
flakes. Process flaked fish, garlic, bread and milk in a food processor until well
combined. With motor running, gradually add olive oil in a thin, steady stream
and continue to process until well combined and smooth, then transfer
mixture to a bowl. Season to taste with freshly ground black pepper and
mix well. Serve warm brandade with sliced rustic-style bread.
Makes about 2 cups. Serves 4-6

Warm brandade and wilted greens sandwiches

1 baguette
Olive oil
1 clove of garlic, bruised
1 bunch of spinach (about 500g), trimmed
1 cup baby rocket leaves
1 quantity warm brandade

Cut baguette on the diagonal into 48 thin slices, brush each slice lightly with olive oil and toast on both sides, then rub one side with garlic.

Heat 2 teaspoons olive oil in large frying pan, add spinach and rocket leaves and toss over medium heat until just wilted. Season to taste with freshly ground black pepper, then remove from heat, drain excess liquid and coarsely chop.

Divide wilted greens among half the toasts, top with heaped teaspoonfuls of brandade and another piece of toast.
Makes 24

Brandade tarts with marlin and capers

2 sheets of frozen shortcrust pastry, thawed
2 pieces of marlin (about 160g each), tuna or swordfish
Olive oil
20g butter
2 tablespoons small capers, drained and
    patted dry on absorbent paper
½ quantity warm brandade

Using a 6-7cm pastry cutter, cut 24 rounds from pastry sheets, then use to line 24 lightly greased 6cm tart tins. Prick pastry bases using a fork, then cover with plastic wrap and freeze for 30 minutes. Place tart shells on an oven tray and bake at 210C for 10-12 minutes or until dry and light golden, then transfer to a wire rack to cool.

Brush marlin with a little olive oil and char-grill over medium-high heat for 2 minutes on each side for rare or until cooked to your liking, then cut each piece into 12 even-sized pieces.

Melt butter in a small saucepan, add capers and cook over medium heat for 2-3 minutes or until crisp, then drain on absorbent paper.

Spoon heaped teaspoonfuls of brandade into tart cases, top each with a piece of marlin and sprinkle with fried capers. Serve immediately.

Makes 24

LAMB MEATBALLS

THIS MIXTURE OFFERS A WEALTH OF IDEAS – THINK COCKTAIL FOOD, PILAF OR A SUPERIOR MEATLOAF

BASE RECIPE

1kg minced lamb
70g (1 cup) soft day-old breadcrumbs
2 eggs, lightly beaten
1 clove of garlic, finely chopped
2 tablespoons chopped flat-leaf parsley
40g (½ cup) grated pecorino or parmesan
Olive oil

Combine all ingredients except olive oil in a large bowl, season to taste and, using your hands, combine well. Use meatball mixture in one of the following recipes or, using slightly damp hands, roll tablespoons of mixture into balls and place on a tray. Heat 1 tablespoon olive oil in a heavy-based frying pan and cook meatballs, in batches, turning frequently, over medium heat for 4-5 minutes or until browned and cooked through, adding more oil if necessary.
Makes about 50. Serves 6-8

Cocktail meatballs with pebronata sauce

1 quantity meatball mixture, formed into balls using
  teaspoonfuls and cooked according to base recipe
Pebronata sauce
¼ cup olive oil
3 shallots, finely chopped
2 teaspoons chopped thyme
2 cloves of garlic, finely chopped
5 juniper berries, crushed
250ml dry red wine
400g can chopped tomatoes
2 fresh bay leaves
2 large red capsicum, quartered, seeded, grilled until
  blackened, peeled and thinly sliced

For pebronata sauce, heat olive oil in a frying pan, add shallots and cook over medium heat for 3 minutes or until soft, then add thyme, garlic and juniper berries and cook for 30 seconds or until fragrant. Pour in wine, increase heat to high and cook for 2 minutes or until reduced and syrupy. Add tomatoes and bay leaves and simmer over medium heat for 15 minutes or until reduced, then add capsicum and cook for another 10 minutes or until of a sauce consistency. Season to taste with sea salt. Makes about 2 cups sauce.
  Serve warm meatballs with warm pebronata sauce for dipping.
Serves 6-8

Lamb and feta meatballs with pilaf

Olive oil
1 onion, finely chopped
1 stick of cinnamon
1 clove of garlic, finely chopped
400g (2 cups) long-grain rice, rinsed
1 litre chicken stock
70g (½ cup) currants
½ cup coarsely chopped coriander leaves
Finely grated rind of 1 lemon
1 quantity meatball mixture (omitting pecorino and
    substituting with 125g crumbled feta)
½ teaspoon ground allspice
¼ teaspoon ground cinnamon

Heat 2 tablespoons olive oil in a large saucepan, add onion, cinnamon stick and garlic and cook over medium heat for 6-8 minutes or until onion is soft. Add rice and stir until rice is lightly toasted, then add stock and currants, season to taste and bring to the boil. Reduce heat and cook, covered, over low heat for 15 minutes or until liquid is absorbed and rice is cooked. Remove from heat, discard cinnamon stick and stir in coriander and lemon rind, then stand, covered, for 5 minutes.

Meanwhile, place meatball mixture, allspice and ground cinnamon in a bowl and, using your hands, combine well. Using slightly damp hands, roll tablespoons of mixture into balls. Heat 1 tablespoon olive oil in a heavy-based frying pan and cook meatballs, in batches, over medium heat for 6-8 minutes or until browned and cooked through, adding more oil if necessary, then serve meatballs with warm pilaf.
Serves 6-8

Lamb and pistachio meatloaf

½ quantity meatball mixture, omitting pecorino
75g (½ cup) pistachios
Tabasco sauce, to taste
400g rindless bacon rashers
Mashed sweet potato or parsnip purée, optional, to serve

Place meatball mixture and nuts in a bowl, add Tabasco to taste and combine well.

Lightly grease a 9x19cm loaf tin, then place bacon rashers, slightly overlapping, to cover base and both long sides of tin, allowing bacon to overhang sides. Spoon lamb mixture into tin and fold bacon over the top to enclose mixture. Cover with foil and bake at 170C for 30 minutes. Remove foil and bake for another 30 minutes or until juices run clear when pierced with a skewer. Drain off liquid and rest meatloaf in pan for 5 minutes before turning out. Serve meatloaf sliced, with mashed sweet potato or parsnip purée, if using.
Serves 4-6

MASHED POTATO

FLAVOUR CLASSIC, CREAMY MASH WITH CAPERS, BAKE IT INTO A PIE, OR MAKE SWEET, SOFT SCONES

BASE RECIPE

1kg floury potatoes, such as spunta, sebago or nicola,
   peeled and halved
100g unsalted butter, chopped
200ml hot milk
Pinch of ground nutmeg, optional

Cook potatoes in boiling salted water until tender, then drain well. Return to same pan and stir over low heat for 1-2 minutes or until potatoes are dry. Add butter and, using a potato ricer or potato masher, mash well. Using a wooden spoon, stir in hot milk and nutmeg, if using, and beat until mixture is smooth and creamy. Season to taste and serve immediately.
Serves 6

For each of the following, add ingredients to 1 quantity hot mashed potato and combine well.

Parmesan mash: 80g (1 cup) grated parmesan.

Caper mash: 45g (¼ cup) salted capers, soaked for 1 hour, drained and coarsely chopped.

Herb mash: ¼ cup finely chopped chives, flat-leaf parsley or dill.

Olive oil mash: Omit milk and butter and add 125ml extra virgin olive oil.

Potato and caraway scones

25g cold unsalted butter, chopped,
  plus extra, for greasing
250g (1⅔ cups) self-raising flour, sifted
2 teaspoons caraway seeds
220g (1 cup) cold mashed potato
½ cup buttermilk, plus extra, for brushing
Unsalted butter and raspberry jam, to serve

Using fingertips, rub butter into flour in a large bowl, then, using a fork, stir in 1½ teaspoons caraway seeds, mashed potato and buttermilk until mixture just forms a soft dough; do not overmix. Turn out mixture onto a lightly floured surface and, using your hands, form into a 16x20cm rectangle. Using a 5cm pastry cutter, cut 12 rounds from dough, pressing scraps together and re-using if necessary. Place scones, 2cm apart, on a greased oven tray, brush tops with extra buttermilk and sprinkle with remaining caraway seeds, then bake at 220C for 20 minutes or until golden. Transfer to a wire rack to cool slightly, then serve warm with unsalted butter and raspberry jam.
Makes 12

Ligurian bean and potato pie

Olive oil
1 clove of garlic, finely chopped
1½ tablespoons finely chopped oregano
350g green beans, trimmed, steamed
    until tender and coarsely chopped
1 quantity warm olive oil mashed potato
3 eggs, lightly beaten
100g fresh ricotta
60g (¾ cup) grated parmesan
70g (1 cup) fresh breadcrumbs

Heat 2 tablespoons olive oil in a frying pan, add garlic, oregano and beans and cook over medium heat for 4 minutes or until garlic is soft. Place bean mixture, mashed potato, eggs, ricotta and parmesan in a large bowl, season to taste, then stir gently to combine. Liberally oil base and side of a 2-litre ovenproof dish, scatter over two-thirds of breadcrumbs, then spoon in potato mixture, smoothing top. Drizzle top of pie liberally with olive oil, sprinkle over remaining breadcrumbs, then bake at 180C for 45 minutes or until light golden. Cool slightly, then serve pie warm or at room temperature.

Serves 6-8 as a light lunch, as an accompaniment to grilled beef or lamb, or as part of an antipasti selection

CHERMOULA

SPIKED WITH HERBS, CITRUS AND SPICES, THIS CONDIMENT PERFECTLY PARTNERS POULTRY OR FISH

BASE RECIPE

1 cup (firmly packed) flat-leaf parsley leaves,
    coarsely chopped
1 cup (firmly packed) coriander leaves,
    coarsely chopped
3 cloves of garlic, chopped
½ spanish onion, chopped
2 fresh small red chillies, seeded
2 teaspoons sweet paprika
3 teaspoons ground cumin
2 teaspoons ground coriander
2 tablespoons lemon juice
½ cup olive oil

Process all ingredients and 1 teaspoon sea salt in
a food processor until a coarse paste forms, then
transfer to an airtight container. Chermoula will
keep refrigerated for up to 3 days.
Makes about 1 cup

Fish tagine

750g skinless firm white fish fillets,
    such as monkfish or flathead, cut into 3cm pieces
½ cup chermoula
¼ cup olive oil
1 large onion, thinly sliced into rings
2 teaspoons ground coriander
1 tablespoon ground cumin
2 teaspoons ground ginger
Pinch of saffron threads
3cm piece of cinnamon stick
1 fresh bay leaf
½ preserved lemon, flesh discarded, skin finely chopped
1½ cups fish stock or water
¼ cup coriander leaves
Couscous tossed with roasted flaked almonds, to serve

Place fish and chermoula in a glass or ceramic bowl
and stir to coat fish well, then cover and refrigerate
for 30 minutes.
    Heat olive oil in a heavy-based saucepan, add onion
and cook over medium heat for 5 minutes or until
translucent. Add ground coriander, cumin and ginger
and stir for 2 minutes or until fragrant. Add saffron,
cinnamon, bay leaf, preserved lemon and stock and
simmer, covered, over very low heat for 10 minutes.
Add fish, cover and simmer gently for 10 minutes or
until just cooked through, then season to taste. Serve
fish tagine scattered with coriander leaves, with almond
couscous passed separately.
Serves 4

Snapper stuffed with prawns and chermoula

1.8kg whole red snapper
8 medium green prawns, peeled and cleaned
½ cup chermoula
1 tablespoon olive oil
Tomato and green olive salad, optional,
    and lemon wedges, to serve

Pat snapper dry with absorbent paper, then, using a small sharp knife, score thickest part of the flesh in a diamond pattern. Place fish on an oiled foil-lined oven tray. Combine prawns with 2 tablespoons chermoula in a small bowl, then place mixture in fish cavity. Spread remaining chermoula over fish, rubbing into cuts and all over to coat well. Drizzle with olive oil and roast at 200C for 30-35 minutes or until fish is just cooked through. Stand for 5 minutes before serving with a tomato and green olive salad, if using, and lemon wedges.

Serves 4

Quail and chickpea salad with chermoula dressing

6 butterflied quail, halved
2 tablespoons za'atar
½ cup olive oil
¼ cup chermoula
2 tablespoons lemon juice
2 cups cooked chickpeas
4 vine-ripened tomatoes, peeled, seeded and chopped
½ spanish onion, finely chopped
80g (½ cup) green olives, pitted and halved
½ preserved lemon, flesh discarded, skin finely chopped
½ cup flat-leaf parsley, coarsely chopped
Rocket leaves, to serve

Place quail in a glass or ceramic dish, sprinkle with za'atar, drizzle with 2 tablespoons olive oil, then turn to coat in mixture and set aside.

Place remaining olive oil, chermoula and lemon juice in a small bowl and whisk to combine. In another bowl, place chickpeas, tomatoes, onion, olives and preserved lemon, add three-quarters of the chermoula dressing and stir to combine well.

Char-grill or barbecue quail, in batches, for 2-3 minutes on each side or until just cooked through, then rest in a warm place for 3 minutes.

Stir parsley into salad, then divide among 4 plates with some rocket leaves. Top each salad with 3 quail halves, then drizzle with remaining chermoula dressing.
Serves 4

WALNUT PESTO

REWORK A VERSATILE CLASSIC USING SWEET WALNUTS, PEPPERY BASIL AND QUALITY PARMESAN

BASE RECIPE

½ cup (firmly packed) flat-leaf parsley leaves
1¼ cups (firmly packed) basil leaves
1 clove of garlic, chopped
60g (¾ cup) grated parmesan
50g (½ cup) walnuts, roasted
⅔ cup extra virgin olive oil, plus extra, to cover

Process all ingredients in a food processor until a coarse paste forms, then season to taste and combine well.

If not serving immediately, transfer pesto to a bowl, pour over enough extra olive oil to just cover and refrigerate, covered closely with plastic wrap, for up to 1 week.

Makes about 1¼ cups

Broad bean, prosciutto, potato and bocconcini salad

400g chat potatoes, scrubbed
500g podded broad beans
   (about 1.25kg in pods)
100g prosciutto (about 8 slices)
½ cup walnut pesto
3 cups (150g) baby rocket
200g cherry bocconcini, torn in half

Cook potatoes in boiling salted water until just tender, cool, then cut into 2-3cm pieces and place in a bowl. Blanch broad beans in boiling salted water for 2-3 minutes, drain and refresh in iced water, then drain again. Peel broad beans and add to potatoes. Place prosciutto on an oven tray and cook under a medium hot grill for 1-2 minutes or until crisp, then cool and break coarsely.

Add pesto to vegetables in bowl and toss gently to combine. Add rocket, prosciutto and bocconcini and toss gently until just combined, then divide among bowls or plates.

Serves 4 as an entrée or light lunch

Pesto, ricotta and artichoke lasagne

600g fresh ricotta
1 egg
½ teaspoon freshly grated nutmeg
¾ cup pouring cream
340g jar artichoke hearts marinated in oil,
   drained and coarsely chopped
1 quantity walnut pesto
300g dried instant lasagne sheets
Green salad, to serve

Process ricotta, egg and nutmeg in a food processor
until smooth, add cream and process until just
combined, then stir in chopped artichoke hearts.
Spread a thin layer of pesto over the base of a 15x25cm
ovenproof dish, then cover pesto with a layer of pasta
sheets, breaking pasta if necessary to fit. Spread
one-third of the ricotta mixture over pasta, then repeat
process twice more with remaining pesto, pasta and
ricotta mixture, finishing with a layer of ricotta mixture.
Cover with foil and bake at 180C for 20 minutes, then
remove foil and bake for another 20 minutes or until
heated through and top is golden. Remove from oven
and stand lasagne for 15 minutes. Serve with a green
salad passed separately.
Serves 6

Boneless leg of lamb roasted with salami and pesto stuffing

1.75kg boneless leg of lamb
80g thinly sliced mild salami
½ cup walnut pesto
25g (⅓ cup) fresh breadcrumbs
1 egg yolk
Steamed chat potatoes and
    green salad, optional, to serve

Unroll lamb leg and place, flesh-side up, on a work surface, then cover flesh with salami slices. Place pesto, breadcrumbs and egg yolk in a bowl, combine well, then spread pesto mixture over salami, re-roll lamb and secure with string at 4cm intervals. Place lamb on rack in roasting pan and roast at 200C for 50 minutes for medium rare or until cooked to your liking. Cover loosely with foil and rest in a warm place for 10 minutes before slicing. Serve with steamed chat potatoes and green salad, if using.

Serves 4-6

BRAISED DUCK

A STAR ON ITS OWN, THIS NOURISHING BRAISE IS A MASTER OF REINVENTION

BASE RECIPE

1 tablespoon olive oil
6 duck marylands
2 onions, halved, thinly sliced
750ml dry red wine
3 cups chicken stock
90g (½ cup) small black olives
1½ tablespoons thyme leaves
1 stick of cinnamon
Steamed green beans and sugar snap peas, optional, to serve

Heat olive oil in a heavy-based flameproof casserole over medium-high heat and cook duck, in batches, skin-side down for 5 minutes or until golden, then turn and cook for another 2 minutes. Remove duck from pan, drain off all but 2 tablespoons of oil, add onions and cook, stirring occasionally, for 6 minutes or until onions are soft. Return duck to pan with wine, stock, olives, thyme and cinnamon, then season to taste and bring to a simmer. Reduce heat to low, then cook, covered, for 70 minutes or until meat is very tender. To use in either of the recipes overleaf, remove duck with a slotted spoon and, if using in duck ravioli, reserve cooking mixture.

   To serve immediately, keep duck warm and transfer cooking mixture to a saucepan; boil over medium heat for 15 minutes or until reduced by half. Serve duck with sauce spooned over, with steamed green beans and sugar snap peas, if using.

Serves 6

Braised duck and potato gratin

1 quantity braised duck
1kg desiree potatoes
12 sage leaves
¼ cup pouring cream
⅓ cup olive oil
Green salad, optional, to serve

Remove meat from duck marylands in large pieces, discarding skin and bones, then coarsely shred. Thinly slice potatoes lengthways into 5mm-thick slices, then place one-quarter of the potatoes, slightly overlapping, in a lightly oiled 20x30cm ovenproof dish.

Scatter potatoes with one-third of the shredded duck meat, then scatter 4 torn sage leaves over duck. Season to taste, then repeat layering twice more, finishing with a layer of potatoes. Drizzle over cream and olive oil, then cover dish with foil and cook at 180C for 40 minutes or until potatoes are tender. Remove foil and cook for another 20 minutes or until golden on top, then serve immediately with green salad, if using.

Serves 4-6

Duck ravioli

½ quantity braised duck
60 8cm-square wonton wrappers
1 egg, lightly beaten
2 cups duck cooking mixture
Thyme sprigs, optional, to serve

Remove meat from duck marylands, discarding skin and bones, then shred finely. Place 10 wonton wrappers on a dry surface and place 1 tablespoon of shredded duck in the centre of each wrapper. Brush edges with beaten egg, then cover with another wrapper and press edges together to seal, removing any air pockets. Using an 8cm fluted pastry cutter, trim ravioli edges. Repeat with remaining wrappers and duck meat. At this stage, ravioli can be refrigerated in a single layer, covered with plastic wrap, for up to 2 days.

Place duck cooking mixture in a saucepan and simmer over high heat for 20-25 minutes or until reduced by one-third and of a good sauce consistency.

Cook ravioli, in 2 batches, in boiling salted water for 2 minutes or until pasta floats to the top. Drain well, then divide among shallow bowls, spoon over a little sauce and serve immediately, topped with thyme sprigs, if using.
Serves 6 as an entrée or 4 as a main course

STEWED BEANS

WHITE BEANS ADAPT TO COUNTLESS FLAVOURS – TRY CHEESY PUREE OR AN OCEAN TROUT STEW

BASE RECIPE

2 tablespoons olive oil

1 onion, finely chopped

2 cloves of garlic, thinly sliced

100g bacon rashers, rind removed, finely chopped, optional

1 teaspoon dried oregano

1 dried bay leaf

300g (1½ cups) dried cannellini beans,
    soaked in cold water overnight, then drained

800ml chicken or vegetable stock

Heat olive oil in a large saucepan, add onion, garlic, bacon,
if using, and oregano, and cook over low heat for 5 minutes
or until onion begins to soften. Add bay leaf, beans and stock,
bring to the boil, then reduce heat and cook over low heat,
stirring occasionally, for 30-40 minutes or until beans are tender.
Season to taste.

Serve stewed beans immediately or at room temperature as
an accompaniment to char-grilled sirloin steak, grilled or roast
lamb, beef or chicken, or as part of an antipasti selection.

Serves 4-6

Cannellini bean and parmesan purée

1 quantity warm stewed beans, omitting bacon
   and bay leaf
Extra virgin olive oil
50g grated parmesan
Shaved parmesan and thin slices of
   toasted ciabatta, optional, to serve

Process beans, ⅓ cup olive oil and grated parmesan in
a food processor until a coarse paste forms. Purée can
be served as a dip, as part of an antipasti selection,
or as an accompaniment to beef or lamb roasts and
stews, or barbecued beef or lamb. If serving as a dip,
serve in a warmed bowl, drizzled with extra virgin olive
oil and scattered with shaved parmesan, with slices of
toasted ciabatta passed separately.

Makes about 4 cups

Cannellini bean, ocean trout and basil stew

1 quantity stewed beans, substituting bacon with
    50g thinly sliced spicy pancetta and omitting
    dried oregano
400g can chopped tomatoes
800g ocean trout fillet, skinned and pin-boned,
    cut into 4cm pieces
⅓ cup (loosely packed) basil leaves, torn,
    plus extra, for sprinkling

Place stewed beans and tomatoes in a large saucepan,
stir to combine well, then bring mixture to a simmer. Stir
in pieces of ocean trout, cover, then cook over medium
heat, stirring occasionally, for 7 minutes or until ocean
trout is cooked but still pink in the middle. Stir in basil
leaves, season to taste, then divide among bowls,
sprinkle with extra basil leaves, and serve immediately.
Serves 4-6

RED CURRY PASTE

AN ESSENTIAL IN THAI CUISINE, THIS PASTE CAN BE USED IN CURRIES AND STIR-FRIES OR AS A MARINADE

BASE RECIPE

12 dried long red chillies, seeded and chopped
6 cloves of garlic, coarsely chopped
5 red shallots, chopped
1 stalk of lemongrass, white part only, chopped
2cm piece of galangal, peeled and chopped
4 coriander roots, washed and chopped
1 teaspoon shrimp paste

Process all ingredients and 1-2 tablespoons water in a food processor until a smooth paste forms, then transfer to a sterilised glass jar. Paste will keep refrigerated for up to 3 weeks.
Makes about 1 cup

Red curry paste-rubbed spatchcock

4 spatchcock (about 500g each), butterflied
⅓ cup red curry paste
100ml coconut cream
2 tablespoons lime juice
¼ teaspoon ground white pepper
3 coriander roots, washed and coarsely chopped
Lime wedges and coriander sprigs, to serve

Rinse spatchcock, pat dry with absorbent paper and place on a large foil-lined oven tray, breast-side up.
  Process curry paste, coconut cream, lime juice, white pepper and coriander roots in a food processor until smooth, then rub mixture over spatchcock, cover and refrigerate for at least 3 hours or overnight. Roast spatchcock on same tray at 200C for 40 minutes or until just tender. Serve halved or quartered with lime wedges and coriander sprigs.
Serves 4

Pork curry

2 cups coconut cream
⅓ cup red curry paste
2 tablespoons fish sauce
65g (¼ cup) grated palm sugar
1 cup coconut milk
600g pork fillet, trimmed and cut into 1cm-thick slices
140g can sliced bamboo shoots, drained
6 kaffir lime leaves, coarsely torn
24 Thai basil leaves
2 fresh long red chillies, thinly sliced on the diagonal
Steamed jasmine rice, to serve

Reserve 2 tablespoons coconut cream, then place
remaining coconut cream in a heavy-based saucepan
and simmer, stirring occasionally, over medium-high
heat for 8-10 minutes or until cream separates. Stir in
curry paste until well combined, then cook over low
heat for 8-10 minutes or until thickened slightly. Stir in
fish sauce and sugar and cook for 5 minutes, then add
coconut milk and simmer for another 5 minutes. Add
pork, bamboo shoots, lime leaves and half the basil
leaves and simmer gently for 10 minutes or until pork
is tender. Serve curry drizzled with reserved coconut
cream, scattered with remaining basil leaves and
sliced fresh chillies, with steamed jasmine rice
passed separately.
Serves 4

Stir-fried beef with red curry and snake beans

2 tablespoons peanut oil
500g beef rump steak, trimmed and
    thinly sliced across the grain
2 cloves of garlic, coarsely chopped
⅓ cup red curry paste
1 tablespoon fish sauce
1 tablespoon grated palm sugar
200g snake beans, cut into 3cm lengths
6 kaffir lime leaves, thinly sliced
24 Thai basil leaves
2 fresh long red chillies, seeded and
    thinly sliced lengthways

Heat oil in a wok or heavy-based frying pan over high heat and stir-fry beef, in 2 batches, for 2-3 minutes or until browned, then remove from pan. Add garlic and stir-fry for 1 minute or until almost golden, then add curry paste and cook for 2 minutes. Add fish sauce and sugar and stir-fry for 1 minute. Add snake beans, lime and basil leaves and browned beef and stir-fry for another 2 minutes or until beans are tender and beef is heated through. Serve immediately, scattered with chillies.
Serves 4

SEASONED CRUMBS

MAKE A REFINED CRUST FOR FISH OR PIE OR SIMPLY ADD CRUNCH TO SNAPPY GREEN VEGETABLES

BASE RECIPE

¼ cup olive oil
1 small onion, finely chopped
1 tablespoon orange juice
1 tablespoon lemon juice
105g (1½ cups) breadcrumbs,
    made from day-old bread
1 teaspoon finely grated lemon rind
2 tablespoons pinenuts,
    roasted and finely chopped
1 tablespoon finely chopped flat-leaf parsley
1 tablespoon currants

Heat olive oil in a small frying pan, add onion
and stir occasionally over medium heat for
5 minutes, then add juices and cook for another
5 minutes or until juices have evaporated. Add
breadcrumbs and stir over low-medium heat
until golden, then remove from heat, stir in
remaining ingredients and season to taste.
    Seasoned crumbs will keep, refrigerated,
in an airtight container for up to 3 days.
Makes about 1½ cups

Zucchini, asparagus and broccoli with chilli and herb crumbs

Olive oil
2 zucchini, sliced on the diagonal
2 heads of broccoli, cut into florets
1 bunch of asparagus, trimmed and cut into 4cm lengths
400g green beans, trimmed
2 teaspoons white wine vinegar
1 quantity seasoned crumbs
1 fresh small red chilli, seeded and finely chopped
Thinly peeled rind of 1 lemon, cut into julienne

Heat 2 tablespoons olive oil in a heavy-based frying pan,
add zucchini and cook, in batches, for 2-3 minutes on
each side or until golden, then drain on absorbent paper.
    Bring a large saucepan of salted water to the boil,
add broccoli and cook for 1-2 minutes, then remove
and plunge into a bowl of iced water. Repeat process,
cooking asparagus and green beans separately for
1-2 minutes or until tender. Drain well, then transfer
to a large bowl with zucchini, add 2 tablespoons olive
oil and vinegar, and season to taste.
    Combine seasoned crumbs with chilli
and lemon rind, then scatter over vegetables
and serve immediately.
Serves 4-6

Baked blue-eye with fennel, olive and rocket crust

2 cups trimmed rocket leaves
4 blue-eye fillets (about 200g each)
1 small bulb of fennel, trimmed and thinly sliced
2 tablespoons chopped black olives
1 quantity seasoned crumbs
80ml dry white wine
2 tablespoons olive oil
Buttered boiled chat potatoes
    and lemon wedges, to serve

Place rocket in a bowl, cover with boiling water and
stand for 2 minutes. Drain, then cool under running
water and drain well, squeezing out excess water.

   Place fish in a baking dish and season to taste. Place
a layer of fennel over each fillet, top with rocket leaves
and olives, then scatter with crumbs, pressing them
firmly over olives and rocket. Drizzle wine, followed by
olive oil, over fish, then bake at 200C for 15-20 minutes
or until fish is tender. Spoon cooking juices over fish
and serve immediately, with chat potatoes and lemon
wedges to the side.

Serves 4

Ricotta and onion torta with roast tomatoes and onion

Olive oil

2 large onions, finely chopped

1kg fresh ricotta

2 tablespoons finely chopped basil

4 eggs

1 tablespoon plain flour

60g parmesan, grated

1 quantity seasoned crumbs

2 large egg tomatoes, coarsely chopped

1 onion, coarsely chopped, extra

2 teaspoons thyme leaves

25g pinenuts, roasted

1 tablespoon coarsely chopped flat-leaf parsley

Heat 2 tablespoons olive oil in a saucepan, add onions and cook for 10 minutes or until soft, then transfer to a bowl and cool. Add ricotta, basil, eggs, flour and parmesan, season to taste and mix well.

Grease a 20cm springform pan, scatter half the crumbs over base, pour in ricotta mixture, then top with remaining crumbs. Cover with baking paper, then bake at 190C for 65 minutes or until puffed. Place tomatoes and extra onion in a small roasting pan, drizzle with olive oil, season to taste, scatter with thyme and place in oven with torta for last 20 minutes of cooking time.

Cool torta to room temperature, scatter with pinenuts and parsley and serve with roast tomatoes and onion.

Serves 6

POACHED CHICKEN

AN EASY ASIAN TECHNIQUE THAT YIELDS MELTINGLY TENDER CHICKEN AND A FLAVOURSOME STOCK

BASE RECIPE

Sliced poached chicken can be served with steamed jasmine rice, stir-fried bok choy and soy sauce for dipping.

1.6kg chicken
4 green onions
2 coriander roots, washed
30g ginger, thinly sliced
¼ teaspoon sichuan pepper
12 black peppercorns

Rinse chicken inside and out. Place remaining ingredients, 1 tablespoon sea salt and 2 litres cold water in a large saucepan or stock pot and bring to the boil. Carefully add chicken, and extra water, if necessary, so it is submerged, return to the boil, then cover with a tight-fitting lid, turn off heat and leave chicken covered for 2 hours; remaining heat will finish the cooking process. Remove chicken from liquid, strain and reserve stock. Chicken and stock can be used in one of the following recipes; check recipe details for specific requirements. Strained stock can be frozen for up to 1 month.
Makes 2 litres chicken stock. Serves 4

White-cooked chicken with ginger-green onion sauce

6 green onions, very thinly sliced, plus extra,
    cut into julienne, to serve
¼ cup finely grated ginger
⅓ cup peanut oil
1 teaspoon sesame oil
1 poached chicken, chopped into 12 pieces
Steamed jasmine rice, to serve

Place green onions and ginger in a small heatproof bowl. Place oils in a small saucepan and heat over medium heat until smoking, then pour immediately over ginger and green onions in bowl and stir in ¼ teaspoon salt. Serve white-cooked chicken, scattered with extra green onion, with ginger-green onion sauce and steamed jasmine rice passed separately.
Serves 4

Bang-bang chicken

2 poached chicken breasts, skin on
150g green mung bean (cellophane) noodles
1½ tablespoons, plus 1 teaspoon extra, sesame oil
75g (¼ cup) Chinese sesame paste
2 tablespoons dark soy sauce
2 tablespoons hoisin sauce
2 tablespoons honey
1 teaspoon chilli oil
1 lebanese cucumber, cut in half lengthways
    and cut into thin strips
3 green onions, cut into thin slices on the diagonal
½ cup coriander leaves

Place chicken breasts on a work surface and gently
pound with a meat mallet or rolling pin several times
to flatten slightly. Remove skin and shred breast meat
using a fork or fingers, then transfer to a bowl.

   Place noodles in a bowl, cover with boiling water
and stand for 10 minutes, then drain well, return to
bowl and toss with extra sesame oil.

   Process remaining sesame oil, sesame paste, sauces,
honey and chilli oil in a food processor and, with motor
running, gradually add ¼-⅓ cup warm water to form
a smooth sauce.

   Place noodles on a large plate, top with shredded
chicken and sliced cucumber and pour sauce over.
Scatter with green onions and coriander, then
serve immediately.

Serves 4

Chicken pho

20g Vietnamese mint leaves

20g Thai basil leaves

20g spearmint leaves

100g beansprouts

4 limes, cut into wedges

200g 5mm-wide dried rice stick noodles

2 poached chicken breasts, skin removed, finely shredded

1.25 litres chicken stock

2 tablespoons fish sauce

Thinly sliced fresh small red chillies, optional, to serve

Place herbs, beansprouts and lime wedges on a large plate and set aside.

Place noodles in a large heatproof bowl, cover with boiling water and stand for 10 minutes or until soft, then drain. Divide hot noodles between 4 warm soup bowls and top with chicken.

Meanwhile, bring chicken stock to the boil in a saucepan, stir in fish sauce, then ladle over noodles and chicken and serve immediately scattered with chillies, if using, with herb and lime plate passed separately.

Serves 4

PORK AND VEAL RAGU

THE SAVOUR OF RAGU PROMISES PIES, PASTA AND LADLEFULS SERVED OVER STEAMING POLENTA

BASE RECIPE

30g butter
¼ cup olive oil
8 sage leaves
2 onions, finely chopped
3 cloves of garlic, finely chopped
2 carrots, cut into 1cm pieces
1 stalk of celery, halved lengthways and cut into 1cm pieces
2 leeks, halved lengthways and thinly sliced
Large pinch of ground nutmeg
1 stick of cinnamon
250ml red wine
500g veal shoulder, trimmed and cut into 2-3cm pieces
500g pork scotch (neck), trimmed and cut into 2-3cm pieces
2 cups beef stock
2 cups tomato passata
1 tablespoon tomato paste
Soft polenta or mashed potato, optional, to serve

Heat butter and oil in a large heavy-based saucepan, add sage leaves,
onions, garlic, carrots, celery, leeks and spices and cook, stirring
occasionally, over medium heat for 10 minutes. Add red wine and cook
for 15 minutes or until most of the liquid has evaporated. Add veal and
pork and cook, stirring occasionally, for 5 minutes, then stir in remaining
ingredients and season to taste. Bring mixture to the boil, then cook,
covered, over low heat for 2 hours, stirring occasionally or until meat
is very tender. Serve with soft polenta or mashed potato, if using.
Makes 2 litres. Serves 6-8

Ragù pies

5 sheets of frozen shortcrust pastry, thawed
½ quantity chilled pork and veal ragù
1 egg yolk, lightly beaten
1 tablespoon sesame seeds
Tomato sauce, to serve

Using an 11cm and a 7.5cm pastry cutter, cut 12 of each sized rounds from pastry sheets, then use large rounds to line a 12-hole (⅓-cup-capacity) muffin tin, pressing firmly to fit. Using a slotted spoon, fill holes with scant ¼ cupfuls of ragù, discarding a little of the sauce if filling is too wet. Brush edges lightly with egg yolk, then top with small rounds of pastry. Press firmly and, using fingers, crimp edges to seal. Brush pie tops with yolk and sprinkle with sesame seeds, then bake at 220C for 10 minutes. Reduce oven temperature to 190C and bake for another 25-30 minutes or until golden and crisp. Serve immediately or at room temperature, with tomato sauce passed separately.
Makes 12

Pork and veal ragù cannelloni

3 16.5x30cm fresh lasagne sheets
30g butter
2 tablespoons plain flour
1 cup milk
⅓ quantity chilled pork and veal ragù
2 cups tomato passata
25g (⅓ cup) finely grated parmesan

Cut each lasagne sheet into 3 equal rectangles. Cook in simmering water for 2-3 minutes or until just tender, then refresh in iced water and drain.

Melt butter in a small saucepan, add flour and stir until a smooth paste forms, then gradually add milk, stirring continuously until mixture simmers and thickens slightly.

Place ¼ cup ragù along one long side of one pasta rectangle, two-thirds of the way down, then fold over to form a log shape. Repeat with remaining pasta rectangles and filling.

Place half tomato passata in base of a 20x30cm ovenproof dish, place cannelloni over, seam-side down, then pour over remaining tomato passata. Spoon white sauce over tomato layer, sprinkle with parmesan and bake at 180C for 30 minutes or until top is golden.
Serves 4 as an entrée

CHOUX PASTRY

MASTER THE ART OF CHOUX FOR CRUNCHY FRITTERS, SAVOURY GOUGERES AND ELEGANT ECLAIRS

BASE RECIPE

Mixture can be used as a base for one of the following recipes or choux pastries can be filled with sweetened cream, mascarpone or ricotta and served dusted with icing sugar.

¼ cup milk
75g unsalted butter, finely chopped
3 teaspoons sugar
125g plain flour
3 eggs

Place milk, butter, sugar and ½ cup water in a small saucepan and cook over medium heat until butter melts and water just comes to the boil. Add flour and stir vigorously over medium heat until mixture comes away from side of pan. Transfer mixture to bowl of an electric mixer and add eggs one at a time, beating well after each.

Use mixture for one of the following recipes or place teaspoonfuls, 5cm apart, on baking paper-lined oven trays and bake at 200C for 20 minutes or until puffed and golden. Turn off oven and cool pastries in oven with door slightly ajar.

Makes about 20 puffs

Eclairs with chocolate glaze and coffee mascarpone

1 quantity choux pastry mixture
1½ tablespoons instant coffee
400g mascarpone
75g icing sugar
100ml pouring cream
100g dark chocolate, chopped
25g unsalted butter

Prepare and cook the choux pastry according to the base recipe, except pipe the mixture into 10cm lengths, 5cm apart, on baking paper-lined oven trays.

Dissolve coffee in 1 tablespoon of boiling water, then, using an electric mixer, whisk coffee mixture, mascarpone, icing sugar and 2 tablespoons cream until soft peaks form.

Using a serrated knife, cut eclairs in half horizontally, taking care not to cut all the way through, then, using a piping bag fitted with a 1.5cm plain nozzle, fill each with tablespoonfuls of mascarpone mixture. Place chocolate, butter and remaining cream in a small heatproof bowl over a saucepan of simmering water and stir occasionally until melted and smooth. Cool for 5 minutes, then spread a little chocolate glaze over the top of each eclair. Place eclairs on a tray and refrigerate for 1 hour or until glaze is set. Serve immediately.

Makes 16

Blueberry and ricotta fritters

1 quantity choux pastry mixture
125g blueberries
125g ricotta, drained
1 litre vegetable oil, for deep-frying
110g (½ cup) caster sugar
2 teaspoons ground cinnamon

Place choux pastry mixture in a bowl, then gently stir in blueberries and ricotta, taking care not to crush blueberries; ricotta will not be smooth. Heat oil in a large heavy-based saucepan or deep-fryer to 160C or until a small spoonful of mixture gently bubbles to the surface; if oil is too hot, the fritters will brown before being cooked in the centre. Fry teaspoonfuls of batter, in batches, for 6-8 minutes or until golden, puffed and cooked through, then drain on absorbent paper. Keep fritters warm in a 150C oven while cooking remaining fritters, then toss hot fritters in combined sugar and cinnamon and serve immediately.

Serves 6

Taleggio gougères

75g butter, chopped
1 shallot, finely chopped
¼ cup milk
125g plain flour
150g taleggio or gruyère, chopped
3 eggs

Melt butter in a small saucepan, add shallot and
cook over medium heat for 2-3 minutes or until soft.
Add milk and ½ cup water and bring mixture just to
the boil, then add flour and stir vigorously over medium
heat until mixture comes away from side of pan. Transfer
mixture to bowl of an electric mixer, add taleggio and
whisk until combined, then add eggs one at a time,
whisking well after each.

   Place teaspoonfuls of mixture, 5cm apart, on
baking paper-lined oven trays, then follow cooking
instructions for base recipe, except leave gougères
in turned-off oven until they are just warm, then
serve immediately.
Makes 20

CHESTNUT PUREE

CHESTNUTS MELT INTO A DENSE, SWEET PUREE – REFINE WITH CREAM, CHOCOLATE OR RICOTTA

BASE RECIPE

1kg fresh chestnuts
3 cups milk
1 vanilla bean, split lengthways
55g (¼ cup) caster sugar

Using a small sharp knife, cut a cross on the flat side of each chestnut and cook in boiling water for 10 minutes, then remove pan from heat. Using a slotted spoon, remove chestnuts a few at a time, wrap in a tea towel and, when cool enough to handle, peel and discard shells and brown skins. (Chestnuts are easier to peel while warm.)

Place peeled chestnuts in a saucepan with milk, scraped seeds from vanilla bean and bean, and bring to the boil over medium heat. Reduce heat to low and cook, covered, for 40 minutes or until milk has been absorbed, stirring occasionally. Remove chestnuts from heat and remove vanilla bean.

Process chestnuts in a food processor until smooth, then place purée in a saucepan with sugar and stir over low heat for 5 minutes or until smooth and thick. Cool. Best used on day of making.

Makes about 3 cups

Mont blanc

1 quantity chestnut purée
300ml double cream, lightly whipped
Coarsely grated dark chocolate, to serve

Press chestnut purée through a potato ricer or mouli onto a large plate, top with whipped cream and sprinkle with coarsely grated chocolate. Serve immediately.

Serves 4-6

Chestnut and chocolate soufflés

20g unsalted butter, melted
2 tablespoons caster sugar, plus extra, for dusting
100g dark chocolate, chopped
¼ cup pouring cream
4 egg yolks
1 tablespoon plain flour
½ cup chestnut purée
6 egg whites
Icing sugar or cocoa, optional, for dusting

Brush eight 200ml ramekins with melted butter and lightly dust with extra sugar, shaking out excess. Place chocolate and cream in a saucepan and stir over low heat until melted and combined. Remove from heat and cool. Add yolks, flour and chestnut purée to cooled chocolate mixture and stir to combine.

Using an electric mixer, whisk egg whites until soft peaks form, then gradually add remaining sugar and whisk until incorporated. Gently fold one-third of egg whites into chocolate mixture to loosen, then fold in remaining egg whites until just combined.

Spoon mixture into prepared ramekins, place on an oven tray and cook at 200C for 10-12 minutes or until risen. Serve immediately, dusted with icing sugar or cocoa, if using.
Serves 8

Chestnut and ricotta cheesecake

125g plain sweet biscuits
60g butter, melted, plus extra, for greasing
2 tablespoons plain flour
450g fresh ricotta
½ cup chestnut purée
110g (½ cup) caster sugar
Finely grated rind of 1 orange
4 eggs, separated
½ cup pouring cream
Whipped cream and marrons glacés, optional, to serve

Process biscuits in a food processor until finely crushed, then add butter and process until just combined. Brush a 22cm round springform pan with extra melted butter, line base with baking paper and dust with flour, shaking out excess. Press biscuit mixture over base of pan and refrigerate for 30 minutes.

Process ricotta in a food processor until smooth, then add chestnut purée, sugar, orange rind and yolks and process until well combined. Transfer ricotta mixture to a large bowl, add cream and stir to combine.

Using an electric mixer, whisk egg whites until soft peaks form, then gently fold egg whites into ricotta mixture. Spoon mixture into prepared pan and bake at 180C for 50-60 minutes or until golden and just firm to the touch. Turn oven off and cool cheesecake in oven for 20 minutes, with door slightly ajar, then remove from oven and cool completely. Serve cheesecake sliced with whipped cream and marrons glacés, if using.

Serves 8

BERRY COMPOTE

LAYER THIS LIME-SPIKED DISH WITH CASSIS CREAM OR FREEZE IT INTO A BRACING YOGHURT PARFAIT

BASE RECIPE

500g strawberries
125g caster sugar
Finely grated rind of 1 lime
1 tablespoon lime juice
120g raspberries
150g blueberries
Thickened cream or Greek-style yoghurt, to serve

Hull strawberries and cut widthways into 3mm slices. Combine sugar, lime rind and juice with 2 tablespoons water in a heavy-based saucepan and stir over low-medium heat until sugar dissolves. Add raspberries and blueberries and stir to coat in syrup, bring to a simmer and cook over low-medium heat, stirring occasionally, for 5 minutes or until soft (raspberries will collapse). Cool to room temperature. Serve compote topped with spoonfuls of thickened cream or Greek-style yoghurt. Compote will keep refrigerated for up to 2 days.
Serves 8

Summer berry and cassis creams

2 eggs, separated
500g mascarpone
1 tablespoon crème de cassis, optional
50g caster sugar
8 sponge finger biscuits
1 quantity berry compote

Using an electric mixer, whisk yolks, mascarpone, liqueur, if using, and half the sugar, until thick. In a separate bowl, using an electric mixer, whisk whites until soft peaks form, then add remaining sugar, whisk until stiff peaks form and fold into mascarpone mixture until just combined. Crumble half a biscuit each into bases of eight 250ml glasses, then divide three-quarters of the compote among glasses and top with mascarpone mixture. Crumble half a biscuit each over mascarpone mixture, then top with remaining compote. Serve immediately or refrigerate for up to 1 day until ready to serve.

Serves 8

Summer berry frozen parfait

1 quantity berry compote
120g caster sugar
8 egg yolks
1 cup thickened cream
½ cup Greek-style yoghurt

Strain compote into a saucepan, reserving berries, then add sugar to compote syrup and stir over medium heat until sugar dissolves.

Meanwhile, using an electric mixer, whisk yolks until very thick, then, with motor running, add hot syrup in a thin, steady stream until well combined. Whisk for another 8-10 minutes or until cooled.

Using an electric mixer, whisk combined cream and yoghurt until soft peaks form, then fold into egg mixture. Process berries in a food processor until coarsely chopped, then fold into cream mixture. Pour into a 10-cup-capacity container and freeze for 3-4 hours. Serve scoops of parfait in bowls or cups.
Serves 8

CHOCOLATE MOUSSE

SMOOTH, SEDUCTIVE CHOCOLATE STARS IN A VELVETY DESSERT OR AS A MORE-ISH CAKE FILLING

BASE RECIPE

200g dark chocolate, chopped
5 eggs, separated
1 tablespoon brandy
¾ cup thickened cream
2 tablespoons caster sugar
Griottines, optional, to serve

Melt chocolate in a heatproof bowl over a saucepan of simmering water, then remove from heat and cool to room temperature. Add yolks and brandy to chocolate mixture and stir to combine. Using an electric mixer, whisk cream until soft peaks form. Using an electric mixer with clean beaters, whisk whites until foamy, then gradually add sugar and whisk until soft peaks form. Fold one-third of the whites into the chocolate mixture, then fold in half the whipped cream. Fold in remaining whites and cream until well combined. Spoon chocolate mousse among six 125ml glasses or ramekins and refrigerate until ready to serve. Serve topped with Griottines, if using. Chocolate mousse will keep refrigerated for up to 2 days.
Serves 6

Frozen chocolate, orange and hazelnut mousse

1 quantity just-made chocolate mousse
100g (⅔ cup) hazelnuts, roasted, skinned
   and coarsely chopped
60g glacé orange peel, finely chopped
Whipped cream, optional, to serve

Combine all ingredients in a bowl, transfer to
a freezer-proof container, cover and freeze for
at least 4 hours or until firm. Serve scoops of
frozen mousse in bowls, with cream, if using.
Serves 6

Chocolate cake filled with chocolate mousse

150g dark chocolate, chopped
185g unsalted butter, chopped,
    plus extra, for greasing
6 eggs
220g (1 cup) caster sugar
225g (1½ cups) self-raising flour
½ quantity chocolate mousse, chilled
Dutch-process cocoa, for dusting

Melt chocolate and butter in a heatproof bowl over a saucepan of simmering water, stirring occasionally until smooth. Cool.

Using an electric mixer, whisk eggs and sugar for 5 minutes or until thick, pale and doubled in volume. Add cooled chocolate mixture and fold in until combined. Sift flour over chocolate mixture and fold in gently. Pour mixture into a greased and paper-lined 11x22cm loaf tin and bake at 180C for 40 minutes or until firm to touch. Remove and stand in tin for 10 minutes before turning out onto a wire rack to cool completely. Using a serrated knife, cut cake in half widthways, then spoon chocolate mousse over base and replace top. Dust with cocoa just before serving.
Serves 8-10

FRUIT CURDS

SPOON CURD INTO PASTRY CASES, FOLD THROUGH CREAMY MOUSSE OR BAKE INTO COCONUT CAKE

BASE RECIPE

6 egg yolks
110g (½ cup) caster sugar
Strained juice and finely grated citrus rind
    of choice (see right)
150g cold unsalted butter, chopped

Whisk egg yolks, sugar and juice in a heatproof bowl over
a saucepan of simmering water until well combined. Whisking
continuously, add butter, one piece at a time, until melted and
smooth, then stir until mixture is thick enough to coat the back of
a wooden spoon. Do not boil. Remove from heat, add rind, if using,
and stir well, then transfer to a bowl, cover closely with plastic
wrap and cool, then refrigerate for 4 hours or until cold. Curd will
keep refrigerated for up to 2 weeks.
Makes about 1⅔ cups

Lime curd: ½ cup strained lime juice
(juice of about 3 limes) and finely
grated rind of 1 lime.

Ruby grapefruit curd: ½ cup
strained ruby grapefruit juice
(about 1 grapefruit).

Passionfruit curd: ½ cup strained
passionfruit juice (pulp of about
12 passionfruit).

Lemon curd: ½ cup strained lemon
juice (juice of about 2 lemons) and
finely grated rind of 1 lemon.

Facing page, curd varieties clockwise
from left: lime, ruby grapefruit,
passionfruit, lemon

Passionfruit mousse

2 egg whites
1 quantity chilled passionfruit curd
300ml thickened cream, whipped to soft peaks
Pulp of 3 passionfruit
Almond bread, optional, to serve

Using an electric mixer, whisk whites until soft peaks
form. Place passionfruit curd in a bowl, fold in half of
the whipped cream to loosen, then remaining whipped
cream and egg whites until just combined. Spoon
mixture into six 1 cup-capacity glasses and refrigerate
for at least 1 hour.

　　To serve, spoon passionfruit pulp among mousses,
then serve with almond bread, if using.
Serves 6

Coconut and lemon curd cake

185g soft unsalted butter, plus extra, for greasing
250g caster sugar
3 eggs
335g (2¼ cups) self-raising flour
125g desiccated coconut
175ml milk
1 cup chilled lemon curd
Icing sugar, for dusting

Grease a 22cm round cake pan and line base and side with baking paper, extending paper 5cm beyond rim of pan.

Using an electric mixer, beat butter, sugar and a pinch of salt in a bowl until light and fluffy, then add eggs, one at a time, beating well after each. Stir combined flour and coconut into egg mixture alternately with milk. Spoon half the batter into prepared tin, spread lemon curd over batter, then carefully spread remaining batter over curd. Bake at 180C for 60-65 minutes or until risen and coming away from side, covering with baking paper halfway through cooking to prevent over-browning. Cool cake in tin before turning out onto a wire rack to cool completely.

Serve cake dusted with icing sugar. Coconut and lemon curd cake will keep, refrigerated, in an airtight container for up to 2 days.

Serves 8

POACHED QUINCE

QUINCE ARE EQUALLY LUSCIOUS JUST AS THEY ARE OR BAKED INTO A TENDER PUDDING OR CAKE

BASE RECIPE

1kg caster sugar
6 small quince (about 250g each)
2 wide strips lemon rind
2 wide strips orange rind
6 cardamom pods
Double cream, optional, to serve

Combine sugar and 1.25 litres of water in a saucepan
and stir over medium heat until sugar dissolves. Peel,
halve and core quince and place in a single layer in
a large ovenproof dish, then scatter with citrus rinds and
cardamom pods. Pour sugar syrup over, then cover dish
tightly with foil and bake at 180C for 2-3 hours or until
fruit is tender and a deep rose pink. Using a slotted
spoon, transfer quince to a bowl, strain syrup over and
discard rind and cardamom pods. Serve warm or chilled
with double cream, if using.
Serves 6

Quince clafoutis

4 eggs
2 egg yolks
110g (½ cup) caster sugar
75g (½ cup) plain flour, sifted
100ml milk
300ml pouring cream
1 teaspoon vanilla extract
8 drained poached quince halves, cut into 2cm pieces
Icing sugar and vanilla ice-cream, optional, to serve

Whisk eggs, yolks and sugar in a bowl until well combined, then add flour and whisk until smooth. Add milk, cream and vanilla and whisk until well combined.

Divide quince among 8 lightly greased 1¼-cup-capacity shallow ovenproof dishes and pour batter over, then place dishes on an oven tray and bake at 190C for 15 minutes or until just set. Serve warm or at room temperature dusted with icing sugar, with a scoop of vanilla ice-cream, if using.

Serves 8

Quince upside-down cake

250g brown sugar
125g soft unsalted butter
3 small drained poached quince halves, sliced
125g self-raising flour
¼ teaspoon baking powder
1 teaspoon ground cinnamon
½ teaspoon ground ginger
2 eggs
⅓ cup milk
Greek-style yoghurt with a few drops of rosewater,
    optional, to serve

Combine 150g brown sugar with 60g butter
in a small saucepan and stir over low heat until
well combined and smooth. Pour mixture into
a well-greased, 20cm round cake tin and place
sliced quince evenly over top.

Sift flour, baking powder and spices into a bowl.

Using an electric mixer, beat remaining sugar with
remaining butter in a bowl until light and fluffy, then
add eggs, one at a time, beating well after each.

Fold flour mixture and milk alternately into butter
mixture until just combined, then spoon mixture over
quince and bake at 175C for 30-40 minutes or until
a cake tester withdraws clean. Stand cake in tin for
5 minutes before inverting onto a plate, then serve
warm or at room temperature, with yoghurt, if using.

Cake will keep in an airtight container for up to 2 days.

Serves 8

SPONGE CAKE

DRESS UP THIS CLASSIC WITH GRAPEFRUIT AND MASCARPONE, OR HONEY, YOGHURT AND ORANGE

BASE RECIPE

Soft butter, for greasing
150g (1 cup) plain flour, sifted, plus extra, for dusting
6 eggs
165g (¾ cup) caster sugar
1 teaspoon vanilla extract
¼ teaspoon finely grated lemon rind

Lightly grease a 22cm springform pan or deep 19cm square cake tin, then dust with extra flour, shaking out excess. Using an electric mixer, whisk eggs and sugar in a large bowl until thick and pale and doubled in volume, then add vanilla and whisk until just combined. Sift one-third of flour over beaten eggs and fold in gently until just combined, then sift remaining flour over, add lemon rind and fold in gently to combine. Pour mixture into prepared pan and bake at 180C for 40 minutes or until golden and centre springs back when lightly pressed. Remove from oven and stand in pan for 10 minutes before turning out onto a wire rack to cool. Sponge cake is best served on day of making.

Serves 8

Cream and jam sponge: Using an electric mixer, whisk 300ml thickened cream, 1 teaspoon vanilla extract and 1½ tablespoons icing sugar until soft peaks form. Split sponge in half horizontally, then sandwich together with 1 cup rhubarb, quince or strawberry jam, and cream mixture. Serve dusted with icing sugar.

Orange sponge with honey yoghurt cream: Follow base recipe, substituting finely grated rind of 1 orange for lemon rind. For honey yoghurt cream, using an electric mixer, whisk 1 cup cream, 1 cup Greek-style yoghurt, finely grated rind of ½ orange and 80ml honey until firm peaks form. Split sponge cake in half horizontally, then sandwich together with honey yoghurt cream.

Facing page, cream and jam sponge

Pink grapefruit and mascarpone trifle

295g (1⅓ cups) caster sugar
300ml freshly squeezed pink grapefruit juice
750g firm ricotta
1 teaspoon vanilla extract
2 eggs
1 tablespoon Cointreau
250g mascarpone
1-day-old sponge cake
3 pink grapefruit, rind removed and segmented

Combine 220g (1 cup) sugar with juice in a small saucepan and stir over low heat until sugar dissolves, then simmer for 5 minutes, remove from heat and cool to room temperature.

Using an electric mixer, beat ricotta, vanilla, eggs, liqueur and remaining sugar in a large bowl until smooth, then stir in mascarpone. Cut sponge vertically into 1cm-thick slices and use one-third to line the base of a 2-litre glass serving bowl or eight 1-cup-capacity bowls, then drizzle one-third of the grapefruit syrup over sponge in base. Spoon over one-third of the mascarpone mixture and smooth, then scatter with one-third of the pink grapefruit segments. Repeat layering twice more, finishing with grapefruit. Cover closely with plastic wrap and refrigerate for at least 30 minutes before serving.
Serves 8

Cabinet pudding

¼ sponge cake
40g (¼ cup) sultanas
2 cups pouring cream
4 eggs
110g (½ cup) sugar
Finely grated rind of 1 lemon
Ground cinnamon and double cream, to serve

Using a serrated knife, cut sponge into 1½cm pieces, then place in the base of a 4cm-deep 1.2-litre ovenproof dish and scatter with sultanas. Whisk cream, eggs, sugar and lemon rind in a bowl until well combined, then pour over sponge and sultanas and stand for 30 minutes. Place dish in a deep roasting pan and pour enough boiling water into pan to come halfway up side of dish, then bake at 180C for 40 minutes or until just set. Stand for 10 minutes before serving warm or cold dusted with cinnamon, with double cream passed separately.
Serves 6

MERINGUES

ETHEREAL BROWN SUGAR MERINGUES SUIT A RANGE OF GUISES, FROM SOFT TO CRUNCHY

BASE RECIPE

2 egg whites
100g brown sugar
½ teaspoon cornflour
Few drops vanilla extract

Using an electric mixer, whisk whites until soft peaks
form, then add 1 tablespoon sugar and beat for
3 minutes or until sugar dissolves. Add remaining
sugar, a little at a time, whisking until sugar dissolves
after each addition, then continue to whisk until mixture
is smooth and glossy. Add cornflour and vanilla and beat
until well combined, then spoon mixture into a piping
bag fitted with 1cm plain nozzle and pipe 3cm rounds
of mixture onto baking paper-lined trays. Bake at 120C
for 45 minutes or until dry and crisp, then stand on
trays until cooled. Meringues will keep in an airtight
container for up to 3 days.
Makes about 40 meringues

Brown sugar meringues with vanilla mascarpone

100g mascarpone
Scraped seeds from 1 vanilla bean
1 quantity meringues
Icing sugar, optional, for dusting

Place mascarpone and vanilla bean seeds in a bowl
and beat with a wooden spoon until well combined
and smooth. Spread a little mascarpone mixture onto
the base of half the meringues and top each with
another meringue. Dust with icing sugar, if using,
and serve immediately.
Makes about 20 filled meringues

Crushed meringues with strawberries and cream

500g strawberries, plus extra, optional, to serve
2 tablespoons kirsch
1½ cups pouring cream
20 meringues

Hull and slice strawberries, then place in a bowl with kirsch, toss to combine and stand for 30 minutes. Using an electric mixer, whisk cream until soft peaks form. Reserve 2 meringues. Coarsely crush remaining meringues and divide among six 1½-cup-capacity glasses or bowls, scatter with strawberries, then spoon over cream. Crumble reserved meringues over cream. Serve immediately, topped with extra strawberries, if using.
Serves 6

Queen of puddings

2 cups milk
40g unsalted butter
210g (3 cups) day-old breadcrumbs
½ teaspoon vanilla extract
2 tablespoons caster sugar
1cm-wide strip lemon rind
4 egg yolks, lightly beaten
180g cherry or strawberry jam, warmed
½ quantity meringue mixture

Place milk and butter in a saucepan, bring to a simmer,
then remove from heat. Add breadcrumbs, vanilla
extract, sugar and rind, combine well and stand for
15 minutes, then remove rind. Stir egg yolks into milk
mixture until well combined, then pour mixture into
a lightly greased 1.5-litre ovenproof dish and bake at
180C for 20 minutes or until lightly golden and just set.
Remove from oven and stand for 5 minutes, then gently
spread jam over pudding, being careful not to break
surface. Spoon brown sugar meringue mixture over
jam and bake for another 5 minutes or until golden.
Serve immediately.
Serves 4-6

FIG PASTE

REDOLENT OF ROSEMARY AND WINE, FIG PASTE PARTNERS CHEESE OR MORPHS INTO SWEET TREATS

BASE RECIPE

400g dried figs, coarsely chopped
125ml red wine or orange juice
60g walnuts or almonds, chopped
2 tablespoons honey
Pinch of ground cloves
1 teaspoon chopped rosemary

Soak figs in 1 cup boiling water for 1 hour, then
combine undrained figs in a saucepan with remaining
ingredients and simmer, stirring frequently, over
medium heat for 25 minutes or until mixture is a very
thick paste. Cool paste, then serve at room temperature
as an accompaniment to cheese (aged cheddar, washed
rind or blue). Fig paste will keep, refrigerated, in an
airtight container for up to 3 weeks.
Makes about 2½ cups

Chocolate fig sweetmeats

1 quantity just-made fig paste
  (made using orange juice)
1 teaspoon finely grated orange rind
150g dark chocolate, finely chopped
Cocoa, for dusting

Remove fig paste from heat, stir in orange rind and
chocolate, stand for 10 minutes or until chocolate
is melted, then stir to combine well. Cool until firm
enough to roll rounded teaspoonfuls into balls.
Refrigerate sweetmeats for 4 hours or overnight,
then dust with cocoa and serve with coffee.
Chocolate fig sweetmeats will keep, refrigerated,
in an airtight container for up to 2 weeks.
Makes about 45

Fig and almond tart

1 quantity cooled fig paste,
    made using chopped, roasted blanched almonds
5 amaretti biscuits, finely chopped
110g (⅔ cup) raisins, chopped
2½ tablespoons chopped glacé orange peel
60g dark chocolate, chopped
½ teaspoon ground cinnamon
2 large (29x29cm) sheets frozen shortcrust pastry, thawed
1 egg yolk, combined with 1 tablespoon water
Whipped cream, to serve

Combine fig paste with remaining ingredients, except
pastry and egg yolk mixture, in a bowl and stir until well
combined. Using 1 sheet of pastry, line base and side
of a 24cm tart tin with removable base, brush edges
of pastry with some of egg yolk mixture, then spoon
fig mixture into pastry case, smoothing surface. Use
remaining pastry sheet to cover filling, pressing pastry
joins to seal where necessary and trimming side evenly.
Brush tart with remaining yolk mixture, prick pastry
several times with a fork, then bake at 180C for
45 minutes or until deep golden. Cool tart to room
temperature, then serve wedges with whipped cream.
    Fig and almond tart will keep, refrigerated, in an
airtight container for up to 3 days.
Serves 6

glossary

AMARETTI BISCUITS: crunchy or soft small Italian-style macaroons based on ground almonds. The hard variety, which also contains ground apricot kernels and almond extract, was used in this book.

ASIAGO: a semi-firm Italian cheese with a rich, nutty flavour. Yellow with tiny holes, it comes in small wheels with glossy rinds and is made from whole or part-skim cow's milk. When young, asiago is used as a table cheese; aged over a year, it becomes hard and suitable for grating.

BAKING POWDER: a raising agent that is two parts cream of tartar to one part bicarbonate of soda (baking soda).

BEETROOT: beets or red beets.

BOCCONCINI: small balls of fresh mozzarella, a delicate, semi-soft white cheese traditionally made in Italy from buffalo milk. Spoils rapidly so must be kept under refrigeration, in brine, for 1 or 2 days at most.

BROAD BEANS: available fresh, dried and frozen. Called fava beans in the USA.

BUTTER: use salted or unsalted (sweet) butter as directed (125g is equal to one stick of butter).

BUTTERMILK: sold alongside other milk products in supermarkets. Low in fat (1.8g fat per 100ml) and with a refreshing, sour tang, it is used in desserts and for baking.

CANNELLINI BEANS: small dried white beans (also available in cans).

CAPSICUM: also known as pepper or bell pepper. Discard seeds and membranes.

CASTER SUGAR: superfine or finely granulated table sugar.

CHERRY BOCCONCINI: tiny balls of fresh mozzarella (see also **BOCCONCINI**).

CHINESE SESAME PASTE: a paste made from sesame seeds. Available from Asian food stores.

COINTREAU: orange-flavoured liqueur from France.

CORIANDER: also known as cilantro or Chinese parsley.

CORNFLOUR: also known as cornstarch; used as a thickening agent in cooking.

CORNICHONS: tiny sour French gherkins.

CREME DE CASSIS: a liqueur flavoured with blackcurrants.

CREME FRAICHE: cultured thick cream with a fresh sour taste. Does not separate when boiled.

CUT INTO JULIENNE: fruits, vegetables or citrus rinds cut approximately 3mm thick in 25mm strips.

DESICCATED COCONUT: unsweetened, dried, shredded coconut.

DUTCH-PROCESS COCOA: 'dutching' is a method of alkalising cocoa. An alkali is added during processing, neutralising the astringent quality of the cocoa and giving it a rich dark colour and smoother, more rounded flavour. Available from specialty food stores and delicatessens.

FONTINA: semi-hard Italian cheese with a nutty flavour similar to gruyère.

GALANGAL: a rhizome resembling ginger in shape but with a pink-hued skin. The flesh is more dense and fibrous than ginger, while the flavour more delicate. Readily available from Asian greengrocers.

GLACE ORANGE PEEL: available from delicatessens and specialty food stores.

GOAT'S FETA: this salty, crumbly cheese is traditionally made from sheep's or goat's milk, though today large commercial producers often make it with cow's milk. It's often stored in brine; if so, rinse it before using to remove some of the saltiness. Use within a few days of purchase and, for best flavour, serve at room temperature.

GORGONZOLA PICANTE: this is the name given to the harder, sharper version of this famous Italian blue cheese; gorgonzola dolce has a sweeter taste and softer texture. Semi-soft and creamy when young, gorgonzola ages into a pungent, crumbly cheese. It usually comes in foil-wrapped wedges cut from medium-sized wheels.

GREEN ONION: an immature onion pulled when the top is still green and before the bulb has formed; sometimes called a shallot or a scallion.

GRIOTTINES: brand name of small, bitter, red cherries that are pitted and macerated in kirsch.

GRISSINI: thin, crisp Italian breadsticks, available from most supermarkets.

GRUYERE: a Swiss cheese with small holes and a nutty, slightly sweet flavour.

HOISIN SAUCE: a thick, sweet and spicy Chinese paste made from salted fermented soy beans, onions and garlic; used as a marinade or baste, or to accent stir-fries and barbecued or roasted foods.

HORSERADISH CREAM: a creamy prepared purée of grated horseradish, vinegar, oil and sugar; some versions have cream added.

ICING SUGAR: also known as powdered sugar or confectioner's sugar.

JUNIPER BERRIES: dried berries that are used to flavour gin, in marinades and also for pickling.

KAFFIR LIME LEAVES: also known as *bai makrut*; these look like two glossy dark green leaves joined end to end, forming a rounded hourglass shape. With their intense fresh citrus flavour, they are used in many Asian dishes, especially in Thai cooking. They are sold fresh, dried or frozen, although the dried leaves are less fragrant, so double the number called for in a recipe if you substitute them for fresh leaves.

KIRSCH: a clear fruit brandy distilled from cherries.

LEBANESE CUCUMBERS: short, slender and thin-skinned; also known as European cucumbers.

LIGURIAN OLIVES: from the Italian Riviera, these are black in colour and high in oil, with a delicate sweet flavour.

MARRONS GLACES: chestnuts that have been poached in syrup and then glazed.

MASCARPONE: a fresh, unripened, smooth triple-cream cheese with a rich, sweet, slightly acidic taste.

MUSHROOM
Dried porcini: dried form of an Italian mushroom, also known as a cep or boletus mushroom. Available from delicatessens. Soften in hot water for 20 minutes before use.
Field: wild version of the common white cultivated mushroom.
Swiss brown: full-flavoured mushroom, also known as roman or cremini. If unavailable, substitute button or cap variety.

PALM SUGAR: also known as *nahn dtan bip*, jaggery, *jawa* or *gula melaka*; made from the sap of sugar cane and palm trees. Sold in a variety of forms, from soft to very hard and from light to dark. If unavailable, substitute brown sugar.

PASTIS: a clear, strong, aniseed-flavoured apéritif from the South of France.

PECORINO: a dry, sharp, salty, sheep's milk cheese.

PERNOD: a yellowish, aniseed-flavoured liqueur from France, distinguished from pastis by its absence of licorice and its lighter taste.

POLENTA: yellow or white coarse granular meal made from maize or corn; also called cornmeal.

POTATOES
Chat: baby new potatoes.
Desiree: pink-skinned potato with creamy yellow flesh. Good for baking, roasting and in salads.
Nicola: creamy, firm-textured potato with yellow flesh and skin. Suits boiling, mashing or roasting.
Sebago: brown-skinned, white-fleshed potato. Suitable for boiling, baking, frying and particularly good for mashing.
Spunta: brown-skinned, yellow-fleshed potato. Suitable for baking, frying, mashing and roasting, but not boiling.

POURING CREAM: also known as fresh or pure cream. It contains no additives and has a fat content of 35 per cent.

PRESERVED LEMONS: lemons preserved in salt and lemon juice. A common ingredient in North African cooking, available from specialty food stores.

RICARD: popular brand of pastis.

ROSEWATER: aromatic extract made from crushed rose petals.

SAFFRON THREADS: the dried stigmas of the crocus flower. Available from specialty food stores, spice shops and some supermarkets.

SELF-RAISING FLOUR: plain flour that is sifted with baking powder in the proportion of 1 cup flour to 2 teaspoons baking powder.

SHALLOTS: also known as eschalots or French shallots. Small golden brown or red bulbs, grown in clusters.

SHRIMP PASTE: also known as *kapi*, *trasi* or *belacan*; a strong-scented, very firm preserved paste made from salted dried shrimp. Used as a pungent flavouring in many South-East Asian soups and sauces. It should be chopped or sliced thinly, then wrapped in foil and roasted before being used.

SNAKE BEANS: long (about 40cm), thin, round, fresh green beans, Asian in origin, with a taste similar to green or french beans. Used most frequently in stir-fries, they are also called yard-long beans because of their length.

SPANISH ONION: a purplish-red onion with a mild flavour.

STAR ANISE: the dried fruit of a Chinese tree. It looks like an eight-pointed star and has a sweet, aniseed-licorice flavour. Used commonly in Asian stocks and marinades.

SUGAR SNAP PEAS: also known as honey snap peas; fresh pods of immature peas which can be eaten whole, similarly to snowpeas (mange tout).

SUMAC: ground spice from a slightly astringent, lemon-flavoured red berry. Available from spice shops and Middle Eastern food stores.

SWEET POTATO: a starchy root vegetable which is available in orange and white varieties.

TALEGGIO: this rich (48 per cent fat) Italian cheese is made from whole cow's milk. Its flavour can range from mild to pungent, depending on its age. When young, its colour is pale yellow and its texture semi-soft. As it ages it darkens to deep yellow and becomes rather runny. Taleggio is sold in flat blocks or cylinders and is covered either with a wax coating or a thin mould.

THAI BASIL: also known as *bai horapha*, this is different from holy basil and sweet basil in both looks and taste. Having smaller leaves and purplish stems, it has a slight licorice or aniseed taste, and is one of the basic flavours that typify Thai cuisine.

TOMATO PASSATA: Italian-style puréed and sieved tomatoes.

TOMATO PASTE: concentrated tomato purée used to flavour soups, stews, sauces and casseroles.

VIALONE NANO: Italian short-grain rice favoured for use in risottos and soups. Available from specialty food stores.

VIETNAMESE MINT: not a type of mint at all, but a pungent and peppery narrow-leafed member of the buckwheat family. Also known as Cambodian mint, *phak phai* or laksa leaf, it is a common ingredient in Thai cuisine.

WASHED-RIND CHEESE: being first surface-ripened by bacteria, then washed, it has an orange or white rind and a strong smell.

ZA'ATAR: a Middle Eastern spice mixture, comprising equal quantities of sesame seeds, thyme and sumac with a little salt. Available from spice shops and Middle Eastern food stores.

ZUCCHINI: courgette.

index

conversion chart

measures

One Australian metric measuring cup holds approximately 250ml, one Australian metric tablespoon holds 20ml, one Australian metric teaspoon holds 5ml. The difference between one country's measuring cups and another's is within a two- or three-teaspoon variance. North America, New Zealand and the United Kingdom use a 15ml tablespoon.

All cup and spoon measurements are level.

We use large eggs with an average weight of 60g.

Unless specified, all fruit and vegetables are medium sized and herbs are fresh.

DRY MEASURES

metric	imperial
15g	½oz
30g	1oz
60g	2oz
90g	3oz
125g	4oz (¼lb)
155g	5oz
185g	6oz
220g	7oz
250g	8oz (½lb)
280g	9oz
315g	10oz
345g	11oz
375g	12oz (¾lb)
410g	13oz
440g	14oz
470g	15oz
500g	16oz (1lb)
750g	24oz (1½lb)
1kg	32oz (2lb)

LIQUID MEASURES

metric	imperial
30ml	1 fluid oz
60ml	2 fluid oz
100ml	3 fluid oz
125ml	4 fluid oz
150ml	5 fluid oz (¼ pint/1 gill)
190ml	6 fluid oz
250ml	8 fluid oz
300ml	10 fluid oz (½ pint)
500ml	16 fluid oz
600ml	20 fluid oz (1 pint)
1000ml (1 litre)	1¾ pints

LENGTH MEASURES

metric	imperial
3mm	⅛in
6mm	¼in
1cm	½in
2cm	¾in
2.5cm	1in
5cm	2in
6cm	2½in
8cm	3in
10cm	4in
13cm	5in
15cm	6in
18cm	7in
20cm	8in
23cm	9in
25cm	10in
28cm	11in
30cm	12in (1ft)

OVEN TEMPERATURES

These oven temperatures are only a guide. Always check the manufacturer's manual.

	°C (Celsius)	°F (Fahrenheit)	Gas Mark
Very slow	120	250	1
Slow	150	300	2
Moderately slow	160	325	3
Moderate	180-190	350-375	4
Moderately hot	200-210	400-425	5
Hot	220-230	450-475	6
Very hot	240-250	500-525	7